ADVANCE PRAISE FO

As someone who has worked with several thousand female entrepreneurs over the last 15 years, I really appreciate Kelly's approach to educating her reader about the Legal Lifecycle of a business. The Q&A format is particularly helpful to the new entrepreneur who needs to find trusted answers quickly. Thank you so much for writing this book!
—Felena Hanson, Founder, Hera Hub

Kelly, I love your new book. The question and answer format makes it easy to understand and even easier to use. Your explanation of the Legal Lifecycle of a business will help our entrepreneurs learn the legal knowledge they need to succeed. A must-have for our busy professionals. Thank you so much!
—Desiree Doubrox, CEO/Founder, An Empowered Woman

Having been a small business owner, investor, and operator for over 30 years, and a small business coach and adviser for just over half a decade, Kelly Bagla nails it. *Go Legal Yourself* provides entrepreneurs an oft-missing but essential ingredient for a successful small business—solid legal input. Good legal advice is expensive. Kelly provides answers to the most-often-asked small business legal questions within the four corners of this gem of a book. If you are starting or running a small business, read it.
—Chuck Sinks, Small Business Coach and Adviser

Kelly Bagla is that rare lawyer able to convey her mastery of business law in plain English. By providing a legal roadmap with signposts identifying the legal questions many don't even know to ask, this book will help entrepreneurs and business owners avoid mistakes and build truly valuable businesses as they navigate the four phases of the business lifecycle.

—Douglas W. Lytle, Business and IP Litigation Attorney

Running a successful business can bring many challenges for even the seasoned entrepreneur. Specifically, legal matters are often shoved aside in hopes that nothing really bad happens. As a business strategist and coach, I provide simple, clear solutions to what can seem to be unsolvable situations. Kelly's book is now my best resource for all things legal—aside from Kelly herself of course. *Go Legal Yourself* is a humorous must-read for any business owner who wants to move to the next phase of their business and be legally prepared when they get there. It answers the questions that you didn't even know that you should be asking and prepares your business to not only survive a legal pitfall, but thrive despite it!

—Valari Jackson, Business Coach, Trainer, Speaker—Fierce Focus Coaching

Delfina,

Thank you for being part of this movement

much love

Kelly

Printed and bound in the United States of America
ISBN: 978-0-9989467-0-2

KELLY BAGLA, ESQ.

KNOW THE LEGAL
LIFECYCLE OF YOUR BUSINESS

I dedicate my very first book to my loving sister-in-law, Surinder Bagla, who taught me how to love the English language.

Your support and love have forever changed my life!

FOREWORD

BY MARK LEBLANC

In your hands, you hold a *remarkable* book written by a spirited author. Kelly Bagla is rare indeed. In fact, her enthusiasm is contagious. Her expertise as a business lawyer makes her uniquely qualified to share her wisdom and insights.

I have been on my own nearly my entire adult life. I had a job once for about six months and was inspired by the two words, "You're fired!" At 22, I made a decision to do whatever it would take to make it on my own in my own business.

For the last 25 years, I have coached small-business owners and independent professionals on how to start and grow a business. While the challenges are many, one specific area often gets pushed to the back burner.

How high you fly is often dictated by how strong your foundation is built. And that includes the critical work of establishing your legal structure. Kelly provides you with what you need to know and what you need to do in order to get your legal ducks in a row when it comes to local, state, and federal legal issues.

Many entrepreneurs and business owners are at risk today due to mishandling or ignoring the legal ins and outs of running a business. In the beginning, your investment is small compared to fixing or defending your mistakes down the road.

Imagine your peace of mind when your assets are protected and your tax obligations are minimized. No owner is immune from legal issues and challenges over the course of running a successful business. Will you be prepared when the time comes?

Every business owner would do well to use Kelly's book as a lighthouse guide. Having the right attorney to lean on in times of challenge or confrontation will keep you on path or help you get back on path if you find yourself in the middle of a legal issue.

Mark

Mark LeBlanc
Speaker, Pilgrim and Author of *Never Be the Same* and *Growing Your Business!*

AGREEMENT WITH RESPECT TO *GO LEGAL YOURSELF*

No…. Not another legal disclaimer… I know what you're thinking. If I weren't an attorney, I'd be thinking the same. But I do have to cover my bum, so do read this agreement and then enjoy this book.

READ THIS. You should carefully read these terms and conditions before accessing or reviewing *Go Legal Yourself*. This is an agreement ("Agreement") between you, the Author, and the Publisher. By accessing or reviewing *Go Legal Yourself,* you acknowledge that you have read, understand, and accept the following terms and conditions. If you do not agree and do not want to be bound by such terms and conditions, do not access or review *Go Legal Yourself.*

1. **License Grant**. Subject to the terms of this Agreement, the Publisher grants to you a nonexclusive, revocable, nontransferable, non-sublicenseable license to use *Go Legal Yourself* solely for your own personal or business purposes.

2. **Restrictions.** Your license for *Go Legal Yourself* and any text, information, graphics, materials or documents (collectively defined as "Content and Materials") therein are subject to the following additional restrictions and prohibitions on use: You may not (i) copy, print (except for the express limited purpose permitted by Section 1 above), republish, display, distribute, transmit, sell, rent, lease, loan, or otherwise make available in any form of by any means all or any portion of *Go Legal Yourself* or any Content and Materials; (ii) use *Go Legal Yourself* or any materials obtained therefrom to develop, or use as a component of, any information, storage and retrieval system, database, information base, or similar resource (in any media now

existing or hereafter developed) that is offered for commercial distribution of any kind, including through sale, license, lease, rental, subscription, or any other commercial distribution mechanism; (iii) create compilations or derivative works of any Content and Materials from *Go Legal Yourself*; (iv) use any Content and Materials from *Go Legal Yourself* in any manner that may infringe any copyright, intellectual property right, proprietary right, or property right of Author, Publisher, or any third parties; (v) remove, change, or obscure any copyright notice or other proprietary notice or terms of use contained in *Go Legal Yourself*; (vi) make any portion of *Go Legal Yourself* available through any timesharing system, service bureau, the internet or any other technology now existing or developed in the future; (vii) use *Go Legal Yourself* in a manner that violates any state or federal laws; and (viii) export or re-export any portion thereof in violation of the export control laws or regulations of the United States.

3. **Copyright.** The content, organization, graphics, design, compilation, magnetic translation, digital conversion and other matters related to *Go Legal Yourself* are protected under applicable copyrights, trademarks, and other proprietary (including but not limited to intellectual property) rights. The copying, redistribution, use, or publication by you of any such matters, except as allowed by Section 1 above, is strictly prohibited. You do not acquire ownership rights to any content, document, or other materials contained in *Go Legal Yourself*. No claim is made to any government-issued forms, agreements, or other content. The copyright to all of the contents in *Go Legal Yourself* and the forms, agreements, checklists is owned by the Author or by third parties from whom the content has been licensed.

4. **Forms, Agreements and Documents.** *Go Legal Yourself* may contain sample forms, agreements, checklists, business documents

and legal documents (collectively, "Documents"). All Documents are provided on a nonexclusive license basis only for your personal one-time use for noncommercial purposes, without any right to relicense, sublicense, distribute, assign, or transfer such license. Documents are provided without any representations or warranties, express or implied, as to their suitability, legal effect, completeness, currentness, accuracy, and/or appropriateness. THE DOCUMENTS ARE PROVIDED "AS IS," "AS AVAILABLE," AND WITH "ALL FAULTS," AND THE AUTHOR AND THE PUBLISHER DISCLAIM ANY WARRANTIES, INCLUDING BUT NOT LIMITED TO THE WARRANTIES OF MERCHANTABILITY AND FITNESS FOR A PARTICULAR PURPOSE. The Documents may be inappropriate for your particular circumstances. Furthermore, state laws may require different or additional provisions to ensure the desired result. You should consult with legal counsel to determine the appropriate legal or business documents necessary for your particular transactions, as the Documents are only samples and may not be applicable to a particular situation. Some Documents are public domain forms or available from public records, but you should check to see if any newer or updated versions have been issued.

5. **No Legal Advice or Attorney-Client Relationship.** Information contained in or made available from *Go Legal Yourself* is not intended to and does not constitute legal advice, recommendations, mediation, or counseling under any circumstance, and no attorney-client relationship is formed. No warranty or guarantee is made as to the accurateness, completeness, adequacy, or currentness of the information contained in *Go Legal Yourself*. Your use and reliance of information in *Go Legal Yourself* is entirely at your own risk.

6. **Indemnification.** You agree to indemnify, defend, and hold the Author and the Publisher and their partners, agents, officers, directors, employees, subcontractors, successors, assigns, third party suppliers of information and documents, product and service providers, and affiliates (collectively "Affiliated Parties") harmless from any liability, loss, claim and expense related to your breach of this Agreement.

7.   **Disclaimer.** THE INFORMATION, CONTENT AND DOCUMENTS FROM OR THROUGH *GO LEGAL YOURSELF* ARE PROVIDED "AS-IS," "AS AVAILABLE," WITH "ALL FAULTS," AND ALL WARRANTIES, EXPRESS OR IMPLIED, ARE DISCLAIMED (INCLUDING BUT NOT LIMITED TO THE DISCLAIMER OF ANY IMPLIED WARRANTIES OF MERCHANTABILITY AND FITNESS FOR A PARTICULAR PURPOSE). *GO LEGAL YOURSELF* MAY CONTAIN ERRORS, PROBLEMS, OR OTHER LIMITATIONS. THE AUTHOR, PUBLISHER, AND THEIR AFFILIATED PARTIES HAVE NO LIABILITY WHATSOEVER FOR YOUR USE OF *GO LEGAL YOURSELF*, EXCEPT AS PROVIDED IN SECTION 8(B). IN PARTICULAR, BUT NOT AS A LIMITATION THEREOF, THE AUTHOR, PUBLISHER, AND THEIR AFFILIATED PARTIES ARE NOT LIABLE FOR ANY INDIRECT, SPECIAL, INCIDENTAL, OR CONSEQUENTIAL DAMAGES (INCLUDING, BUT NOT LIMITED TO, DAMAGES FOR LOSS OF BUSINESS, LOSS OF PROFITS, LITIGATION, OR THE LIKE), WHETHER BASED ON BREACH OF CONTRACT, BREACH OF WARRANTY, TORT (INCLUDING NEGLIGENCE), PRODUCT LIABILITY, OR OTHERWISE, EVEN IF ADVISED ON THE POSSIBILITY OF SUCH DAMAGES. THE NEGATION AND LIMITATION OF DAMAGES SET FORTH ABOVE

ARE FUNDAMENTAL ELEMENTS OF THE BASIS OF THE BARGAIN BETWEEN AUTHOR, PUBLISHER, AND YOU. *GO LEGAL YOURSELF* WOULD NOT BE PROVIDED WITHOUT SUCH LIMITATIONS. NOTHING IN *GO LEGAL YOURSELF* SHALL CREATE ANY WARRANTY, REPRESENTATION, OR GUARANTEE NOT EXPRESSLY STATED IN THIS AGREEMENT.

8. **Limitation of Liability.**

(a) The Author, Publisher, and any Affiliated Party shall not be liable for any loss, injury, claim, liability, or damage of any kind resulting in any way from (a) any errors in or omissions from *Go Legal Yourself*, or (b) your use of *Go Legal Yourself*.

(b) THE AGGREGATE LIABILITY OF THE AUTHOR, THE PUBLISHER, AND THE AFFILIATED PARTIES IN CONNECTION WITH ANY CLAIM ARISING OUT OF OR RELATING TO *GO LEGAL YOURSELF* SHALL NOT EXCEED THE COST OF *GO LEGAL YOURSELF*, AND THAT AMOUNT SHALL BE IN LIEU OF ALL OTHER REMEDIES WHICH YOU MAY HAVE AGAINST THE AUTHOR, THE PUBLISHER, AND ANY AFFILIATED PARTY.

9. **Miscellaneous.** This Agreement shall be treated as though it were executed and performed in San Diego, California, and shall be governed by and construed in accordance with the laws of the State of California (without regard to conflict of law principles). Any cause of action by you with respect to *Go Legal Yourself* must be instituted within one year after the cause of action arose or be forever waived and barred. All actions shall be subject to the limitations set forth in Section 7 and Section 8. The language in this Agreement shall be interpreted as to its fair meaning and not

strictly for or against any party. Any rule of construction to the effect that ambiguities are to be resolved against the drafting party shall not apply in interpreting this Agreement. If any provision of this Agreement is held illegal, invalid, or unenforceable for any reason, that provision shall be enforced to the maximum extent permissible, and the other provisions of this Agreement shall remain in full force and effect. If any provision of this Agreement is held illegal, invalid, or unenforceable, it shall be replaced, to the extent possible, with a legal, valid, and unenforceable provision that is similar in tenor to the illegal, invalid, or unenforceable provision as is legally possible. The Author's or the publisher's failure to enforce any provision of this Agreement shall not be deemed a waiver of such provision nor of the right to enforce such provision. The title, headings, and captions of this Agreement are provided for convenience only and shall have no effect on the construction of the terms of this Agreement.

10. **Arbitration.** Any legal controversy or legal claim arising out of or relating to this Agreement and *Go Legal Yourself* shall be settled solely by confidential binding arbitration in accordance with the commercial arbitration rules of JAMS, before one arbitrator. Any such controversy or claim shall be arbitrated on an individual basis, and shall not be consolidated in any arbitration with any claim or controversy of any other party. The arbitration shall be conducted in San Diego, California. Each party shall bear its own attorneys' fees. Each party shall bear one-half of the arbitration fees and costs incurred through JAMS. The arbitrator shall not have the right to award punitive damages or speculative damages to either party and shall not have the power to amend this Agreement.

DO NOT ACCESS OR REVIEW *GO LEGAL YOURSELF* UNLESS YOU UNDERSTAND AND AGREE WITH THE FOREGOING AGREEMENT.

WHY WRITE THIS BOOK?

I love what I do.

Yes, I am an attorney who loves what she does.

I love helping business owners protect their hard work. There is one thing that every business owner has in common – we know the pains and heartaches of running a business, and if we're lucky, we can eventually become successful. But wouldn't it be nice to know from the inception of your business how to run it successfully? There is so much misleading information out there that business owners too often rely upon, and that information usually ends up hurting the business rather than helping it.

I see this happening too often, so I thought it was time to set the record straight.

Go Legal Yourself is a guide for business owners that explains the four phases of the Legal Lifecycle of your business and how to set up your business for success from day one. This book is written in a way that answers frequently asked questions by business owners. By providing a legal perspective to those questions, I'm hoping to put you in a better position to really understand your business and become more successful by doing so. You will learn what you thought was right, what you should know, and what you never thought of asking. By knowing exactly where you are in your Legal Lifecycle, you can easily move from one phase to another, be it from Startup to Growth or from Establishment to Exit.

Knowing your business Legal Lifecycle is key to running a successful business and puts you at an advantage for less failure, more growth, and overall good business sense.

I have always lived up to my favorite quote. All entrepreneurs should strive to do the same:

"Why blend in when you were born to stand out?"
—Guru Granth Sahib

TABLE OF CONTENTS

INTRODUCTION

KNOW THE LEGAL LIFECYCLE
OF YOUR BUSINESS

**"Entrepreneurship is living a few years of
your life like most people won't, so you can spend
the rest of your life like most people can't."
—Unknown**

Did you know every business has a Legal Lifecycle? Even yours. As a business owner, this is probably the last thing on your mind, but my legal experience has repeatedly shown that business owners who pay attention to the Legal Lifecycle of their business are usually the successful ones.

Wouldn't it be nice for the business Gods to walk you through the Legal Lifecycle of your business and show you the correct way to start, run, manage, and exit your business? What is the likelihood of that? That is why God created business attorneys, or in your case, this book.

From the moment you make the decision to set up your business, you are automatically starting the Legal Lifecycle of your business. By reading this book you will learn the four phases of that Legal Lifecycle and how to better position your business for success. Each phase has its own challenges and rewards. Knowing that your business has:

- A startup phase
- A growth phase
- An established phase, and
- An exit phase

provides you with a road map as to where your business is at any given time. As your business grows and develops, so do your business goals, objectives, priorities, and strategies. Knowing exactly where you are in your business can be the fine line that makes or breaks your business.

Some businesses start fast, grow fast, and fail or succeed fast. Others start small and stay small by design. Many businesses start slowly, then build fast, grow faster, buy other companies, or get sold and molded into larger organizations. But every business has its own Legal Lifecycle.

This book is designed to help you determine where your business is in its Legal Lifecycle and how to get to the next stage. As a business attorney, I have helped many business owners like you move from one stage to the other, and with every stage come new risks and rewards. With every stage also come new legalities to face. This book addresses important questions that:

- You think you know the answers to
- You should know the answers to, and
- You never thought of asking

Educating yourself about the Legal Lifecycle of your business will position you as a better business owner and help you create a successful business.

The 4 Phases of
The Legal *Lifecycle*
of Your Business

PART ONE
STARTUP PHASE

CHAPTER ONE

WHAT ENTITY SHOULD I BE?

"Starting a business is a lot like jumping out of an
airplane and assembling the parachute on the way down."
– Unknown

As a business attorney who helps business owners with their day-to-day legal needs, I frequently hear owners say they have a startup and would like to grow their business. I ask them to define what they mean by being a startup, and the answer usually is, "Well, I have an idea, and I want to protect it," or "I just left my job, and I want to start my own business." Business owners create their own definitions of what a startup is, so it would be helpful for us to understand what a startup is in the legal world.

WHAT IS A STARTUP?

The dictionary defines a startup as "the action or process of setting something in motion." This is not helpful to the newly formed business. The reality is that there is no one definition any two entrepreneurs or business owners agree on. Most say a startup is determined by its age, growth, revenue, profitability, or stability. Neil Blumenthal, co-CEO of Warby Parker, defines a startup as: "a company working to solve a problem where the solution is not obvious and success is not guaranteed." Another entrepreneur, Adora Cheung, CEO of Adora, stated: "A startup is a state of mind. It's when people join your company and are still making the explicit decision to forgo stability in exchange for the promise of tremendous growth and the excitement of making immediate impact."

The best definition of a startup was provided by Alyson Shontell while she was the editor-in-chief of *Business Insider US*. "A startup is an emotional roller coaster that can either result in massive failure or success, after which one's bank account total may either drastically increase or decrease. The person behind a startup is a founder, an often very bright, somewhat crazy person who finds a normal 9-to-5 job dull and is deluded into believing he or she can change the world by working tirelessly in front of a computer screen. The relentless work has been known to shave a few years off a founder's life while adding premature gray hairs, but it can be very rewarding both emotionally and financially for those who pursue it."

Now that we have somewhat of a definition of what a startup is, let's go back to the client who has an idea and wants to protect it, or the client who just left a job and wants to open his or her own business. In both cases, we start with answering the same question—the number one most frequently asked question by business owners in the startup phase:

WHAT ENTITY SHOULD I BE?

The question that should be asked is: What type of business do I want to run?

When starting out, it is important to determine what form of business will work best for your specific situation. The legal structure you choose for your business is one of the most important decisions you will make in the startup process. Your choice of structure can greatly affect the way you run your business, impacting everything from liability and taxes to control over the company. Choosing the right business entity allows an entrepreneur to reduce liability exposure, minimize taxes, and ensure that the business can be financed and run efficiently. It also provides business owners with a mechanism for ensuring that the business operations will continue, rather than be automatically terminated, upon the death of an owner.

When choosing a business entity, you should consider the following:

- Are your personal assets at risk from liabilities arising from your business?
- Are you able to offer ownership to key personnel?
- What are the continued costs of operating and maintain your business?

The most common and simplest form of business is a sole proprietorship. Many small business owners launch their companies as sole proprietorships, in which they and their businesses are essentially one and the same. An individual proprietor owns and manages the business and is responsible for all business transactions. Sole proprietorships have many advantages. They are quick and easy to set up, they do not require large amounts of money, and accounting is relatively simple. However, sole proprietorships have many disadvantages as well.

The biggest disadvantage is that there is no separation between the business assets and the owner's assets. This means that anyone who sues the business for any reason can take away the business owner's cash, car, or even his or her home. Another big disadvantage occurs if the sole proprietorship wants to borrow money. Because there is no separation between business and personal assets, many sole proprietors have to use their personal assets—such as their home—as collateral for a loan. If the business fails and the owner does not have enough money to pay off the loan, the lender can take the owner's home and sell it to get the money back. Needless to say, this type of ownership is the riskiest and, to make things worse, the courts do not see any difference between a sole proprietorship and its owner. So, when the owner passes away, the business ends.

Other forms of business ownership include general and limited partnerships, which consist of two or more partners who are all responsible for the business. They share assets, profits, liabilities, and management responsibilities for running the business. While general partnerships provide a means of raising capital more quickly and allow several people to combine resources and expertise, several problems commonly occur, among them: partners having different visions or goals for the business, an unequal commitment in terms of time and finances, and personal disputes. Some advantages of a general partnership are: shared financial commitment, the ability to pool resources, and—generally—limited startup costs. Some disadvantages of a general partnership include: partners are generally personally liable for business debts and liabilities. Each partner may also be liable for debts incurred by decisions made and actions taken by the other partners.

Changing a sole proprietorship or a general or limited partnership to a corporation or a limited liability company can offer a range of advantages. Most notable is asset protection: a corporation or a limited liability company protects the owner's personal assets in case debts or legal judgments are claimed against the business. Some other advantages are:

Easier to sell

Corporations or limited liability companies are generally much easier to sell and are usually more attractive to buyers than a sole proprietorship. This is because a new buyer will not be personally liable for any wrongdoing on the part of the previous owners. If someone buys a sole proprietorship, the new owner can be held personally liable for any mistakes or illegalities on the part of the prior owner, even if the new owner had nothing to do with those activities. This is usually not the case with a corporation or a limited liability company.

Easier to raise capital

When you are looking to raise money through investment or borrowing, a corporation or a limited liability company makes finding and getting the money easier. If you want to take on investors, you simply sell shares, or stock, or units; and if you want to borrow from banks, the lenders are more likely to loan you money because your business assets can be held as collateral.

Tax savings

When you incorporate, you have numerous tax advantages that are virtually impossible for a sole proprietorship to tap.

Perpetual existence

When you incorporate, you create a separate and distinct legal entity. This separate and distinct entity can exist almost forever, irrespective of what happens to the shareholders, directors, or officers. Corporations have unlimited life.

Privacy and confidentiality

The incorporated form of business is a great way to keep your identity and business affairs private and confidential. If you want to start a business but would like to remain anonymous, a corporation or a limited liability company is the best way to accomplish this.

Increases credibility

Most people feel more secure and confident dealing with a corporation or a limited liability company as opposed to a sole proprietorship. Having an "Inc." or "LLC" after your company's name adds a touch of professionalism and credibility to your business dealings.

Now that we know some of the major advantages of being incorporated, it would be helpful to understand exactly what a corporation and a limited liability company are.

Corporation:

The law regards a corporation as a legal entity that is separate and distinct from its owners. Corporations enjoy most of the rights and responsibilities that an individual possesses; that is, a corporation has the right to enter into contracts, loan and borrow money, sue and be sued, own and sell property, hire employees, own assets and pay taxes, and sell the rights of ownership in the form of stocks.

Corporations are used throughout the world to operate all kinds of businesses. While their exact legal status varies somewhat from jurisdiction to jurisdiction, the most important aspect of a corporation is the limited liability protection. This means that shareholders have the right to participate in profits but are not held personally liable for the company's debts.

There are several different types of corporations, including "C" corporations, "S" corporations, and A Professional Corporation. There are many differences between them, and to really understand which one is right for you requires a conversation with professionals who understand your business.

To establish a C corporation, several requirements and formalities need to be addressed. For example, a corporation needs to issue shares to shareholders. In addition, state requirements usually include minutes be taken at shareholder and board of director meetings, officers be appointed, and specific records be maintained as outlined by the state in which the incorporation documents are filed. The shareholders have ownership in the corporation, the board of directors governs the business, and elected officers manage the day-to-day activities. Corporations must adhere to corporate tax laws and file corporate taxes regularly.

An S corporation is initially formed in the same manner as a C corporation, by filing incorporation documents with the state of incorporation. Once the business has incorporated, the owners may decide to file as an S corporation by filing IRS form 2553. This does not create a separate type of corporation but changes the tax structure of the corporation.

Limited Liability Companies (LLC):

A limited liability company (also known as an LLC) is a unique business entity that allows the owners to limit their personal liability while enjoying the simplicity of pass-through taxation (whereby the profits and losses of the LLC pass directly through to the owner).

Under an LLC, the members are protected from personal liability for the debts of the business, as long as it cannot be proved that the members have acted in an illegal, unethical, or irresponsible manner in carrying out the activities of the business.

When deciding to set up a new entity for your startup, you should consider your startup's financial needs, risk, and the ability to grow. Here are some factors to consider:

- **Complexity** – How complex is your business and what entity best addresses your needs?

- **Liability** – Is the entity you are forming protecting your personal assets from your business assets?

- **Taxes** – Will this entity provide the best tax benefits for your business?

- **Control** – Who will have control over your business, and how do you maintain the majority control?

- **Capital investment** – Will you need outside investment
  money to start and run your business?

- **Licenses, permits, and regulations** – Will the licenses and
  permits be held in the name of your business?

WHAT'S AFTER INCORPORATING?

Once the business is formed, ninety percent of business owners
think they can now enjoy the limited liability protection afforded
by their corporation. Little do they know that they must observe
corporate formalities in order to enjoy that protection. When I
meet with new clients that are already incorporated, I ask to review
their corporate documents to make sure they are observing corporate formalities. Ninety percent of the time, the business owners
do not know what these corporate formalities are or what the law
requires them to do. This leads me to the question that business
owners do not know they should ask. Unasked, it could cost them
their limited liability protection.

Question you don't know to ask: After I form my company, am I
personally protected?

Every business is subject to liabilities. Essentially, you want any such
liabilities to be the responsibility of the company and not result in personal liability to you. However, if you have taken the time and effort
to incorporate your company, then you will likely be protected to a
significant degree from such personal liabilities.

Many business owners, however, are under the mistaken impression that they are completely protected from personal liability by filing Articles of Incorporation (to establish your corporation) or Articles of Organization (to establish an LLC). The act of incorporating your business does not alone afford you liability protection. There are certain actions you must take in order for you and your company to enjoy limited liability protection under the law.

Corporate compliance: You need to treat the incorporated entity completely separate from yourself. In most cases, you may only be one person running the show, but the law requires you to treat the company as if it is a completely separate entity from you. Failure to file required paperwork can lead to fines and penalties, including suspension of your incorporated entity. This paperwork is key to keeping your company in good standing with the state where you incorporated. If your business happens to be sued, the person suing you may try to show that you haven't maintained your business to the letter of the law, thus piercing your "corporate shield" and attaching your personal assets as part of a judgment. Below is a general overview of what you should to do to keep your business in compliance. Of course, specific requirements will vary based on your business type and location:

1. File an annual report – Most states require some sort of annual report filing on the anniversary of your incorporation date.

2. File amendments for any changes – If you make major changes to your corporation, you may need to keep your state up to date with an Articles of Amendment form. Examples of change include: changes to the company name, changes to the registered

agent, changes to the business address, an increase in the number of authorized shares, and changes in business activities.

3. Keep up to date with any meeting minutes – If your business is a corporation, you'll need to record meeting minutes whenever you hold a corporate meeting. The bare minimum are the annual minutes, which appoint directors and officers.

4. File a DBA for any name variations – A lot of times, a business has an official name and then uses any number of variants of that name or in some cases uses different names. In these cases, you should file a DBA (Doing Business As) with the county where you are doing business for each name used.

5. You must obtain a Federal Tax ID number, also known as an Employer Identification Number (EIN), because the incorporated company is now its own separate entity. The EIN acts as the Social Security number for your company.

6. You will need to open a separate bank account for your incorporated entity that has its own checks and its own credit cards.

7. The name of the corporation should be used in full, including "Inc." or "LLC" on all contracts, invoices, and documents used by the corporation. This clearly indicates the existence of the corporation as a separate entity.

8. Always use your title, which means that you will sign on behalf of the corporation, using the name of the corporation and your title.

KEY POINTS:

▶ Every business is different, but every business needs limited liability protection, so try to stay away from sole proprietorships and general partnerships that afford no to little liability protection. The risk of personal liability for the debts and obligations of business are too great.

▶ Choosing the right entity for your company could be the single biggest decision you make as a business owner. First weighing the pros and cons of each kind of business entity will serve you well.

▶ Limited liability protection is not automatic. You can lose that protection very easily, so follow your state's compliance laws.

CHAPTER TWO

NOW THAT I'M INCORPORATED, WHAT'S NEXT?

S tarting a business can be overwhelming, and not knowing what you need is even worse. Incorporating an entity is the easy part; running your business like a business is the hard part. Over the years, I have been contacted by business owners who have just incorporated and don't know what to do next or business owners who are now ready to sell their product or service and don't know what agreements they need. The second question most frequently asked by business owners in the startup phase is:

NOW THAT I'M INCORPORATED, DO I NEED ANYTHING ELSE?

Question that should be asked: What contracts do I need for my business?

The business environment is full of agreements between businesses and individuals. While oral agreements can be used, most businesses use formal, written contracts. Contracts are legally binding agreements and are involved in almost every aspect of your business life. Contracts are essential for business dealings because they are binding on all parties. If one party doesn't hold up its end of the bargain, the other party has legal remedies for damages. A contract serves as a guide to the agreement that must be followed by both parties. It presents each party with the opportunity to:

- Describe all obligations they are expected to fulfill
- Describe all obligations they expect the other party to fulfill
- Limit any liabilities
- Set parameters, such as a time frame, in which the terms of the contract will be met
- Establish payment terms
- Establish all the risks and responsibilities of the parties

What types of contracts you need will vary depending on the nature and the lifecycle of your business. However, common contracts that most businesses in the startup phase require and should have are:

Promissory Note
One of the greatest concerns for any startup is money. Where do you get the money to start your company, and where do you get the money to keep your company going? The four most common sources of startup capital are:

- Personal savings
- Family and friends
- Cash flow from the business
- Credit cards

When using personal savings or money from family and friends, some startups treat this money as a loan that the startup intends to pay off. A promissory note is a loan agreement that allows the company and the individual giving money to record the loan and the terms under which it will be governed, such as the interest rate, payment terms, maturity date, etc. Having a promissory note in place acts as a record for the terms between the parties, as memory could fade and you forget what was agreed to. It also shows you are treating your company as a separate entity and not as your personal piggy bank, which could cost you your limited liability protection.

Client Contract

It does not matter what type of business you are running; for the most part, you should use a contract with customers or clients. This will allow you to control the deal and remain protected if disputes arise between you and your customers or clients. If your business provides services, then you will need a template Client Contract, which you can amend for every new client. The Client Contract will clearly set out the services you provide, an expected start and completion date, the fees you will charge, and how and when you expect to be paid. A detailed Client Contract, which sets out exactly what the client will receive, can help avoid disputes between you and your client, and save you a lot of time and money in the long run. It needs to be noted that there is no such thing as a "standard contract," as this is more myth than reality; too often people simply sign on the dotted line without reading or negotiating the terms of the contract. Every case is different, and care should be taken to make sure you are using the correct Client Contract for your business.

Sales Contract

If your business is involved in selling goods, you will need a Sales Contract that your customers can sign. The Sales Contract lays out important terms and conditions for the sale of goods or products. Here are some important terms to potentially address in your Sales Contract:

- Price: Make sure that the Sales Contract correctly states the price and any discounts, installation charges, and delivery charges.

- Taxes: Try to ensure that the purchaser is responsible for all sales taxes.

- Payment and credit terms: Make sure to state when payment is due.

- Warranties: Decide what warranties you want to give. Typical warranties state that for a designated period, the goods sold will be free from defects of workmanship and will conform to designated specifications. Any necessary repairs will be under warranty for that designated time period.

- Disclaimer: State clearly in your Sales Contract that no other warranties exist, express or implied.

- Liability limitations: Use the Sales Contract to attempt to limit your liability under the contract.

Employment Contract

An Employment Contract is a document both you and your employee sign that dictates the terms of your professional relationship. A well-drafted Employment Contract addresses the following key issues:

- The job description, title, role, and responsibilities
- Whether the employer can change your position at the company
- The length of the agreement
- The salary, bonus, and benefits
- Whether the employee gets stock or stock options in the company
- When the employee can be terminated
- Severance payments, if any
- The employee's responsibilities
- The employee's confidentiality obligations
- Where and how disputes will be handled

Independent Contractor Contract:

You may decide not to hire employees but choose to have independent contractors work on certain projects. If you hire independent contractors to perform services for your business, it is important that you and the contractor understand your rights and responsibilities in the contracting relationship. Misunderstandings can occur, such as the contractor thinking the work he/she has performed belongs to the contractor, or the contractor holding himself/herself out as an employee of your business, which could lead to your business incurring liability and possibly legal action against you.

Each state has its own laws relating to contracts; you should consult with a business attorney to make sure you are entering into the right contracts with the right people.

For a free "Go Legal Yourself!" checklist of must-have contracts, visit www.BaglaLaw.com/GLYcontracts.

Question that you don't know to ask: How should you prepare for when you get sued?

It's not a matter of *if* but a matter of *when* you get sued. There is some risk of a legal action inherent in any business venture. However, it is not always clear what those risks are, and some businesses are at higher risk for litigation than others. Businesses can face lawsuits from employees, customers or clients, and third parties, to name a few. The first step in minimizing that risk is for your contracts to address how litigation will be handled and how to limit the amount of damages, if any.

Contracts are critical to any business, and having a legally drafted contract may save your business a lot of money. Even if you do everything right, there is still a chance your business will be confronted with a lawsuit at some point. Businesses use contracts to safeguard their resources.

For an added layer of protection, it is always advised and is good practice for your business to retain general liability insurance from a reputable insurance company. Once you have incorporated, your second order of business should be to determine your specific insurance needs based on the nature of your business. What risks must be covered? How much coverage will be sufficient? While shopping for insurance, you will want answers to several key questions, such as:

- What are the deductibles?
- Are the coverage limits high enough?
- What items or occurrences are excluded from coverage?
- Are there any gaps in my coverage?

In today's litigious society, liability insurance is more essential than ever. This type of insurance can protect you from lawsuits resulting from:

- Any bodily injuries that occur on your premises to customers, employees, vendors, or visitors
- Injuries sustained as a result of the actions or negligence of one of your employees
- Property damage caused by your employees

There are many different types of insurance that may apply to your particular situation, so before you sign with an insurance company, understand which one or ones are right for you.

KEY POINTS:

▶ Treat your business as a business by using customized contracts and knowing which contracts are a must-have for your business.

▶ Get professional contracts drafted by a business attorney, which can limit your liability and risk when dealing with employees, independent contractors, clients, and vendors.

▶ Invest in additional protection for your company by purchasing general liability insurance.

CHAPTER THREE

SHOULD I TRADEMARK MY LOGO?

B usiness owners spend a lot of time and money designing the logo for their business. Creating a memorable logo and brand is a powerful way to help your business stand out in the mind of your customers and helps them remember your business more easily. So why wouldn't you want to protect that expensive logo?

Talking to clients over the years about their business name or business logo, I have found that they are not concerned about protecting the name or logo, or they feel they can protect it down the road sometime. They think that since they are using the name and logo, it belongs to them and no one else can use that name or logo. This could not be further from the truth. When you spend money on having a professional logo created for your business and tell the world that that logo represents your business, then why not protect it? The third most frequently asked question by business owners in the startup phase is:

SHOULD I TRADEMARK MY LOGO?

Question that should be asked: How do I protect my brand?

A brand is a name, term, design, or symbol that distinguishes your product or service from other products and services so that it can be easily recognized, communicated, and marketed effectively.

A great logo can be like gold to your small business. It acts as your calling card, summarizing your company's beliefs, culture, and quality without the need for any further explanation. That's why it's important to protect your logo from being copied, mimicked or knocked off by lesser brands without your permission, a crime otherwise known as trademark infringement.

There are several ways for you to protect your brand. Here are the most common:

Secure your domain name

Obtaining a domain name for your website is one of the most cost-effective ways to protect the identity of your brand.

Trademark your brand

A trademark is defined as "a word, phrase, symbol, or design, or a combination of words, phrases, symbols, or designs that identifies and distinguishes the source of the goods of one party from those of others." Here are the top five reasons why trademarking your logo is important to your business:

1. Trademarks are among your most valuable business assets. Trademarks are your company's intellectual property and can be given a value separate from other assets in your company. The more your business reputation grows, the more valuable your brand will be. Someday, your trademark could be worth a lot of money.

2. Trademarking your logo will provide you with nationwide protection of your mark. This means you are the only business that may use your mark nationwide in connection with your goods or services. This is especially important in an era when many goods are offered for sale through websites nationwide.

3. As a registered trademark owner, you can bring suit in federal court for trademark infringement and prohibit others from using your mark.

4. A registered trademark builds your brand and allows you to be easily identified and distinguished in the marketplace, as the marketplace is crowded. Trademarks make it easy for customers to find you.

5. Your trademark will not expire as long as you are using it for commerce in the United States. Some of the most recognized brands in the United States today have been around for more than a hundred years. Mercedes was first registered in 1900. Pepsi-Cola was registered in 1896. Today those trademarks are worth billions of dollars.

Copyright your brand

A copyright protects the author of published or unpublished original works, including literary or artistic works plus certain other types of intellectual property. The primary goal of copyright law is to protect the time, effort, and creativity of the creator. As such, the Copyright Act gives the copyright owner certain exclusive rights, including the right to:

- Reproduce the work
- Prepare derivative works (other works based on the original work)
- Distribute copies of the work by sale
- Display the work publicly

In business, the employer typically owns the copyright for any works that the employees create pursuant to their employment with the company. The protection afforded by a copyright guards against the use of the material without the consent of the author.

Patent your brand

A patent is a property right that gives the holder the exclusive right to exclude others from the manufacture, use, or sale of the product or invention. Patenting your brand only makes sense if you have invented something unique and revolutionary; then you'll want to get a patent. A patent can be granted to an inventor to exclude others from making, using, offering for sale, or selling the invention.

Question that you don't know to ask: What makes a good brand name trademarkable?

Trademarks help a company instill brand loyalty and control customer perceptions, so what makes a good trademark? There are generally five categories of trademarks.

1) **Generic**

   The first category refers to generic brand names that identify an entire group or class of products. These are the weakest names and generally cannot be trademarked, names such as "Computer,"

"Milk," "Bread," "Wine," and "eBook." These words cannot be legally protected because they are far too generic.

2) **Descriptive**

Descriptive names are a step above generic but are still hard to protect. A descriptive brand name simply adds a descriptor in front of a generic word. Examples of descriptive names are "Pizza Hut" and "General Motors."

3) **Suggestive**

Suggestive names stand a much better chance of earning legal protection. These are names like "Amazon" and "Greyhound." These names are highly correlated with something else and draw on the power of analogy. They may be more difficult to market but are certainly easier to protect.

4) **Fanciful**

Fanciful names are the easiest to protect and trademark legally because they are unique. These names are created, invented or coined by the brand itself. These are extremely popular in the tech world, such as "Google," "Twitter," and "Xerox."

5) **Arbitrary**

These are brand names that may seem generic but are actually capable of being trademarked because they are obviously used out of context. For example, "Shell" (the oil company) is able to trademark the name "Shell" because it is unrelated to seashells. Another example is "Apple" (the computer company) is able to trademark the name "Apple" because the company is not in the business of selling fruit.

31

When choosing a brand, keep in mind that the brand should be:

- Easy to say and spell
- Memorable
- Extendable – has room for growth
- Positive in feeling
- Does not translate to something negative internationally
- Available from the trademark and domain perspective
- A meaning that has relevance to your business

KEY POINTS:

▶ Put some thought into creating your brand, as it will be your business's calling card.

▶ Your brand is everything to your company; that is how your customers find you. Trademark your logo early to make sure it is secure from others using it.

▶ Protect your overall brand, not just the logo, as your brand will become an asset of your company that could be worth a lot of money someday.

A STORY OF CAUTION FOR STARTUP COMPANIES

What happens when your startup doesn't have its legal ducks in a row? You lose $500,000.

As business owners, we are so focused on running the business that we forget to get our legal ducks in a row. Why does it matter? Think about how much you have always wanted to run your own business and how hard you have worked to become your own boss. Now think about how you need money to run your business and keep the doors open. You ask family and friends, and they can't help you. You ask your bank for a loan or a line of credit, and the bank turns you down. Through a lot of heartache, you finally find a private investor who is willing to listen to your story and invest in your business. Here's what can happen if you don't have your ducks in order.

I received a call one day from a client who was very excited about a business investment. This startup was going to be the first in its space to create software that every business eventually would need and buy. This startup needed $500,000 to finish the software, and my client was going to make the investment. Before any money changed hands, we needed to make sure my client's investment would be secure. I sent our due diligence list to the startup asking for corporate documents and ownership percentage for my client. The startup had no corporate documents and no ownership structure.

Due to the lack of information, the startup looked less desirable to my client. As any prudent investor would, my client decided not to invest, as the startup was not ready. The startup lost its hard work, hopes, and dreams—not to mention $500,000. This happens more often than you think because business owners don't know what they don't know and fail to prepare for these types of situations. To avoid this happening to you, get your legal ducks in a row.

When business owners choose to form a corporation or a limited liability company, they must file the proper formation papers with their home state and any other states in which they are registered to do business. The states then essentially grant the right to conduct business as a legal business entity with all the advantages that it brings. To maintain this right, the business becomes subject to a host of business laws and requirements. These include appointing a registered agent, making timely filings of required forms, and paying fees and franchise taxes.

As long as businesses comply with all these requirements, they are designated as being in good standing with the state they are formed in, and enjoy all the rights and privileges of that state's business laws. However, entities that do not stay on top of their compliance obligations can lose their Certificate of Good Standing. The business then will be considered delinquent, void, suspended, or dissolved. Losing your good standing status can lead to serious consequences, such as:

Possible loss of access to the courts
This may be the most serious consequence, and one that many businesses are not aware of. In many states, a company that is not in good standing may not bring a lawsuit in that state until good standing is restored.

Personal liability

This is the second most serious consequence. The ability to protect your personal liability is no longer available to you; your personal assets can be attached by creditors of the company. If your company is not in good standing, the state can hold individual owners of the company personally liable for conducting business on behalf of the company while it was in a revoked status. These penalties can be severe and levied on each officer, director, or employee who knowingly acted on behalf of the noncompliant company.

Difficulties in securing capital and financing

Most lenders view a loss of good standing as an increased risk and may not approve new financing for the company.

Tax liens

If a company does not pay its franchise tax, and loses its good standing status, the taxing authorities can place a tax lien on the company and possibly the owners of the company. Again, lenders will not generally loan money to companies that have tax liens attached to them, as tax liens take priority.

Fines and penalties

Some states impose fines and penalties on companies that do not comply with the requirements to maintain a Certificate of Good Standing. These can add up quickly and become a burden on the company.

The primary reasons a company loses its good standing status are:
- It lets annual reports or franchise tax obligations lapse.
- It doesn't keep annual minutes.
- The owners don't treat the company as a separate entity.

When you are considering incorporating your business, make sure you do your homework and consider taking the following steps:

1. Get advice from a good certified public accountant.
2. Get help from a good business attorney.
3. File the paperwork and pay franchise taxes as required.
4. Obtain the necessary licenses and permits.
5. Have sufficient capital to run your business.

PART TWO
GROWTH PHASE

CHAPTER FOUR

I'M GROWING TOO FAST; WHAT SHOULD I DO?

"I have a friend who's always jumping from one
opportunity or business to another. To him, the
grass is always greener on another field. He's
never learned that if you water and fertilize the
grass on your own field, it will get greener, and
you'll want to stay. Sometimes the grass truly is
greener somewhere else, but that's only because
someone is over there taking care of it! Take care
of the grass on your own field. If you're con-
vinced you've found your field of dreams, build
it! Stop looking for something better and stay
focused on the opportunity at hand. If you do,
eventually it will become so fresh and desirable
that others will want to play on your field."
– Billy Cox

The focus of your business changes as it moves beyond the startup
phase and into the second phase of your business's Legal Lifecycle,
the growth phase. The growth phase can mean so many different things
to a business owner, and it can be measured by multiple indicators.
Let's first define what growth is.

What is Growth?

The business dictionary defines growth as: "A phase in the lifecycle of an industry when companies move beyond the startup phase into a phase of increased competition for market share." Another definition provided by the business dictionary is "The process of improving some measure of an enterprise's success. Business growth can be achieved either by boosting the top line or revenue of the business with greater product sales or service income, or by increasing the bottom line or profitability of the operation by minimizing costs."

Whether you have a hair salon business with a few employees or a software development company with annual revenue in the millions, both companies are likely to face the same common problems at similar stages in their development. The number one question that business owners in the growth phase ask me is:

I'M GROWING FAST; WHAT SHOULD I DO?

Question that should be asked: How do I protect my fast-growing business?

As an entrepreneur, you dream of the day when you've got a steady stream of customers or clients eager to work with you. But what happens when the workload becomes more than you can handle? As far as problems go, this might sound like a great one to have. But too much growth can actually be bad, especially for startups. Rapid, uncontrolled business expansion can have negative repercussions in the short- as well as the long run. In fact, the result is often the same—failure.

You might be thinking, this makes no sense. It sounds counterintuitive, because businesses exist to make more money and grow with the passage of time. While expansion is always good, what smart business owners and entrepreneurs should look and strive for is "controlled expansion."

Through helping business owners with their growth phase, I have accumulated a list of seven signs that indicate your business is growing too fast, and things might be getting out of control. These are some of the most common problems associated with startups trying to grow too fast. It is essential to know these signs because uncontrollable expansion is the easiest way to go out of business.

Sign One: Your business expenses outweigh your revenue

When money going out of your business is more than the amount coming in, you know you're in trouble. Rapid expansion can lead to cash-flow problems because a growing business incurs growing business costs. When a business expands, so do its expenses. If the cash going out of your business exceeds what's coming in, you might be forced to borrow and take on debt, which is never a good thing. Ideally, all business expenses should be paid through revenue.

Sign Two: There are a growing number of customer complaints

An increasing number of customer complaints and negative feedback are signs that you might have to step back and reassess how you are doing business. A small business with a small number of customers can easily provide individual attention to each customer and produce tailor-made solutions. When a business grows, it may be forced to cut corners, resulting in more customer complaints.

Sign Three: Your employees are overworked and unhappy

If your business is growing uncontrollably, naturally a large proportion of that burden will be borne by your employees. To keep up, they might find themselves working late. This usually results in a dip in productivity and a rise in employee turnover, both of which can negatively affect your business. You may find yourself busy hiring and training new staff when other, more important aspects of your business need your attention.

Sign Four: Your suppliers and vendors can't keep up

Oftentimes when a business grows too quickly, suppliers and vendors get caught off guard and may not be able to keep up with the increased demand. In such cases, it might be a good idea to add to your list of suppliers or get in touch with suppliers who might be better able to cater to your needs.

Sign Five: Your infrastructure, systems and processes can't keep up

Rapid growth can render your business processes and systems useless due to lack of proper infrastructure. Your current software might not be adequate, and old hardware systems may not be able to cope with the increase in demand. Hence, you'll have to invest in better software and hardware solutions.

Sign Six: You start losing customers or clients

Customer or client retention is essential to any business. Your business's ability to keep existing customers or clients while adding new ones is a benchmark of success. If your customers or clients feel they are not being given proper attention, their complaints are not being handled properly, and that there is a dip in the quality of your products or services, you might end up losing them. This will negatively affect business expansion, and it might be time for you and your team to step back and see how you can do a better job.

Sign Seven: Other oversights

Here are some other signs of rapid growth that you might neglect to address:

- You need to buy equipment quickly.
- You're making operational decisions on the fly.
- Your financials are both exhilarating and terrifying.
- You're really uncertain of your next steps.
- You're branching out into foreign territory.

New business owners have numerous goals when they're starting out, including growth. There are ways to reach growth milestones that can help catapult a business to success, but the main focus should always be on reducing your risks, which are attached to the growth milestones. Here are some risks and solutions related to milestones that will help you grow your business or prepare it for growth in the right way:

Milestone One: Hire the right people

Before you can even think about your company's growth trajectory, you need to ensure that you have a solid staff that can help you achieve it. Having the right employees is critical to the success of any business. Good employees can follow instructions, present new ideas, and motivate other employees to work hard. They are dedicated, conscientious, trustworthy, and do not need to be micromanaged. Conversely, the wrong employees can not only slow down or impede the progress of your business, but also can cause you to lose money through wasted training time, improperly performed tasks, and even stealing. Furthermore, any incompetence or improper activities by your employees can reflect poorly upon you and your business.

Before hiring anyone, you should familiarize yourself with the laws and regulations imposed regarding soliciting and interviewing employees. Protecting employee rights, ensuring physical safety, and maintaining fair treatment are at the heart of most laws created to safeguard the hiring process. Laws protect against discrimination on the grounds of race, color, religion, national origin, age, sex, or disability. They also protect against sexual harassment and unfair treatment of employees. You not only need to be aware of such employment laws; you also can protect your business by establishing appropriate policies.

Reducing the Risk: Have the right contracts in place

When hiring employees, a business needs a number of documents in order to reduce its risk. Some of these must-have documents are:

- Employee Handbook, which is always kept up-to-date with changes in the law.

- Nondisclosure Agreements, to keep your trade secrets from being shared with the world.

- Employee Application, which will save you time gathering background information.

- Employee Agreements, which define the professional relationship between you and your employees.

- Invention Assignment Agreements, so any inventions that your employees create while working for your company will belong to your company.

- Independent Contractor Agreements, which help secure the work you just paid for and assure that the work product belongs to your company.

Establishing appropriate company policies will help reduce the risk of litigation.

Milestone Two: Never take your eye off the money

When your business is smaller, you probably have a pretty good command of your numbers. You're able to watch your cash and know quickly how expenses are stacking up to sales. But once you start growing, it becomes harder to keep track of your financials; there are a number of financial implications you need to take into consideration. Start with understanding your cash flow and then creating a budget for your business.

Reducing the Risk: Hire Professionals

Money will always be the telltale of your business. That is why it is extremely important to hire the right accountant. You need someone who knows how to work with fast-growing businesses and can provide you with profit and loss statements, so you know where your business stands at all times. Your accountant will be privy to confidential information and may have access to your bank accounts. When hiring this person, you will need to have an independent contractor agreement or a services agreement in place, which will include confidentiality language. You may want this person to provide you with evidence of liability insurance, which is an additional security measure for your money.

Milestone Three: Collecting your money

A big challenge fast-growing companies can face is that their accounts receivable accumulate faster than their sales or their ability to collect. The company's growing, but it is selling on account and not collecting fast enough.

Reducing the Risk: Have a solid contract in place

Having a solid contract with your customers or clients is critical for a fast-growing business. The contract should lay out the terms of when and how you will get paid. First of all, make sure you have the right payment terms. Next, make sure phrasing in the contract protects your business and gets you paid in a timely manner. If using your customer's or client's contract, beware of language that promises payment after the invoice is approved. This means you could wait months for someone to approve an invoice. Make sure the contract also has language that allows for charging rush fees and passing along costs associated with delays caused by the customer or client. The faster you grow, the more money you will need. Having a solid contract in place can help reduce the risk that you will fall behind on collections.

Now that we have addressed some of the problems that can occur with fast-growing companies and how better to position yourself for such growth, let's address the most important question—one that you would not know to ask.

Question that you don't know to ask: How do I put accountability processes and procedures in place?

Often as a business owner, you become so focused on bringing products or services to market and advertising them, you fail to grow all aspects of the business. As a result, while the business is growing in sales, the infrastructure is not keeping pace with business growth. Flaws in management systems begin to show, and quality control is not in sync with the growth. Eventually, you reach a tipping point in which these flaws cause the system to collapse.

To avoid this collapse you must grow your organizational structure in proportion to your business. Consider the following:

Create a scalable management model

As your business grows, you must develop scalable management and quality-control systems. In the beginning, management and quality control are easy, as everyone knows what everyone else's role in the company is. As your business grows and duties become more segmented among new employees, you must put a management structure in place to ensure accountability against established benchmarks as well as to make sure quality control of your goods and services remains constant. Each position's duties and responsibilities should be defined in writing. An organizational chart should be created that defines who is responsible for what, who reports to whom, and how often.

Define a quality-control system

As your company grows, you must ensure that the quality of your goods or services is maintained despite its increasing size. You must determine what elements belong in a quality-control system and then assign the responsibility of maintaining that quality to someone within your management model.

You should have the following in place to ensure your business is growing in the right way, with the right procedures and the right oversight:

- Hire a really good business attorney
- Employ a really good accountant
- Use a reputable payroll company
- Create internal policies on hiring and firing employees
- Set a company culture and lead by example

KEY POINTS:

▶ Every business wants to grow. Be smart and grow in the right way, so you achieve success and not failure.

▶ Plan for growth; don't just stumble across it. Planning will result in success.

▶ Hire professionals who can help with the growth of your business. Don't try to do it all by yourself. You don't know what you don't know. This is the best single act you can do for your company to ensure success.

CHAPTER FIVE

How Do I Stay On Top Of My Business?

Now that you have learned how to grow your business in the right way, your next step should be to make sure your growing business continues to grow. This is an important part of your business's Legal Lifecycle because growth is key to the survival of any business, and a growing company can quickly fail if the right steps are not taken.

Businesses that do not grow stagnate and eventually die. According to a study carried out by the British economic historian Leslie Hannah in 1999, of the 100 largest US firms in 1912, 29 had, by the time of the study, gone bankrupt; 48 had disappeared; and just 19 of them were still in the US top 100. In the current era of rapid changes, growth must be equally rapid or the opportunity will be lost as competitors gain the advantage. As mentioned above, rapid growth can afford you multiple opportunities, but the rapid growth must be controlled.

The second most frequently asked question by business owners in the growth phase is:

HOW DO I STAY ON TOP OF MY BUSINESS?

Question that should be asked: How do I manage my fast-growing business?

No business can afford to leave its growth to chance. Businesses need a consistent plan that incorporates their vision for growth. Fast growth is not always easy to handle, but a proactive, step-by-step approach can help make it more manageable. It is essential, even in a boom period, that you keep control of the situation. Here are some steps you can take to manage your business:

Define your growth objectives

Your business objectives are the results you hope to achieve and maintain as you run and grow your business. As a business owner, you are concerned with every aspect of your business and need to have clear goals in mind for your company. Having a comprehensive list of business objectives creates the guidelines that become the foundation of your business. Consider some of the following growth objectives you should spend time defining:

- Profitability – Making sure that revenue stays ahead of the costs of doing business.

- Productivity – Investing in employee training, equipment, and the overall resources your company needs for growth.

- Customer Service – Good customer service helps you retain clients and generate repeat revenue. Keeping your customers happy should be a primary objective of your company as you grow.

- Core Values – Your company mission statement is a description of the core values of your company. It is necessary to create a positive corporate culture.

- Marketing – Understanding your consumer buying trends, anticipating product needs, and developing business partners that help your company improve its market dominance.

Other steps that can help manage your business:
- Analyze your sales, overhead, receivables, inventory, and assets.

- Ensure that your growth is sustainable.

- Prepare a growth strategy that takes risks and opportunities into account.

- Forecast your cash requirements.

- Control costs.

- Control debt.

- Line up the refinancing you may need.

As they work hard to manage their fast-growing business, more often than not, business owners forget to ask themselves, "What could go wrong?" This leads me to the question that all business owners should be asking.

Question that you don't know to ask: As I grow, what pitfalls do I avoid?

If you start the growth phase in your business, it is usually because you've done something right. A new product or service has been launched, marketing has been effective, the sales are coming in, and you are delivering efficiently. So, what could possibly go wrong?

At some point in your business—usually when all is going smoothly—you will encounter certain pitfalls. If you want to give your business the best chance of success, it's important to be aware of the most common mistakes and how to avoid them. Knowing the potential pitfalls in advance and understanding how to mitigate them can be the fine line between success and failure.

Here are some common pitfalls I counsel my clients to avoid:

Failure to use professionals

Most business owners mistakenly believe they can do everything on their own. They do everything from writing their own contracts to doing their own accounting, handling clients, and finding new deals. This mind-set is a huge mistake because, although tackling each project on your own is a good way to learn the ins and outs of your business, in the end, all you are doing is crippling your progress, your productivity, and, ultimately, the success of your business. Learn to hire professionals, such as a business attorney and an accountant, put together a management team, and delegate the work to efficient people better skilled in those areas, so you can do what you do best—run your company.

Insufficient capital

In order to function, businesses need money, and a good amount of it. Startups usually have trouble finding funding or attaining credit. Typically, they use the owner's personal financial resources to make ends meet. More experienced companies usually suffer from insufficient capital when spending starts to outweigh revenue. Keep a handle on your capital situation by monitoring your cash flow. The earliest stages of your company's growth are the most vulnerable to insufficient capital, so watch your numbers closely.

Losing key employees

Loss of key employees can occur in many ways. They can quit, they can retire, they can move out of town, or they can die. Your business could suffer significantly if any of these occur and you have no procedures or descriptions of the tasks that key employees perform. To avoid such disaster, consider putting the following in place:

- Create operations manuals.

- Write job descriptions.

- Document extraordinary tasks.

- Cross-train.

Spreading your management team too thin

It's very easy for a fast-growing company to assign too many tasks to the management team. Before you know it, the management team is stretched too thin. Having a simple plan and being able to prioritize and supervise your management team at a higher level can control the pressure on your team. Provide your team a clear plan, with each item assigned to someone. List time lines or milestones for that person to follow. Give everyone involved a copy of the plan so they all stay on track and accomplish the tasks assigned to them before taking on more tasks.

You must plan for these risks and always have a backup plan.

KEY POINTS:

▶ Spend time defining your growth objectives and set goals to achieve them. Rushing into things can catch you off guard and set you back financially.

▶ Do your homework on what could possibly go wrong while you are growing your business—and plan for such pitfalls.

▶ Hire the right professionals to help you with your business. As I have said before, you don't know what you don't know. Don't try to save a few dollars by doing it yourself. This is the worst thing you can do for your business. Be smart and delegate.

CHAPTER SIX

How Do I Keep Going?

As you are growing and managing your growth, understanding where your business is in the growth cycle is vital to your ability to make informed decisions for the company's future. After all, it is impossible to determine where you should be going if you do not know where you are. The third question most frequently asked by business owners in the growth phase is:

How do I keep growing?

Question that should be asked: How do I take my business to the next level?

When you first started your business, you probably did a lot of research. You may have sought help from advisors; you may have gotten information from books, magazines, and other available sources. You invested a lot in terms of money, time, and sweat equity to get your business off the ground. Now what?

Those who have survived startup and are successfully managing their growing business may be wondering how to take the next step and grow the business beyond its current status. There are numerous possibilities; choosing the proper one for your business will depend on the type of business you own; your available resources; and how much money, time, and sweat equity you are willing to invest all over again.

Here are activities some of my successful business owner clients have conducted to address the next steps in the growth state and keep moving forward:

Set goals

Goal setting can be a great way to clarify your focus, measure progress, and track achievements. Creating a business plan or even single targeted tasks can help your business reach new levels of success.

Commit to continuous learning

No matter how much you achieve, there will always be more you can learn and apply for even greater success. Advancing your knowledge and continuing to learn will help your business continue to thrive.

Learn how to delegate

Whether you have employees or subcontractors, learning how to delegate effectively can be the difference between reaching new heights and burning out. Like all business owners, you are accustomed to doing a variety of things yourself, so it can be challenging to identify necessary tasks and assign the work to someone else. By delegating, you will have more time to dedicate to what you do best: grow your business.

Focused on taking their business to the next level, many business owners overlook one important thing—continuing to protect the business brand as the business achieves higher levels of success. Brands today are generally recognized as a key asset creating value for your business. So why are business owners still paying so little attention to developing brand value for their growing business?

Question that you don't know to ask: How do I protect the brand of my growing business beyond the first trademark?

Trademarking your business name at the launch of your company isn't an umbrella to protect future logos, product names, marketing slogans, and other branding assets. Each brand asset needs its own trademark registration. As your business grows, so should protection of your brand. Developing a brand image should not be your last priority, to be addressed only after your business is established.

Your brand image should be developed in parallel with your business, and the branding strategy should constitute an integral part of your business plan. What is the use of making major investments into developing quality goods and services if that quality reputation cannot be captured and developed in the form of your brand image? It is through your brand image that your business will attract and retain customer or client loyalty for your goods and services.

Continuing to develop your brand image requires time, effort, and commitment, and certainly some financial resources, but not as much as you might expect. It is a wise investment to make for your company.

KEY POINTS:

▶ Growing your company in the right way takes some time and thought. Sit down with your team and strategize the best way to achieve your goals.

▶ As you develop new products and services, protect them through trademarks, as one trademark will not protect all of your products and services.

▶ Establish a brand that can be recognized by your customers or clients. One day that brand will be one of your biggest assets, potentially worth a lot of money.

A STORY OF CAUTION FOR GROWTH COMPANIES

There are many stories about businesses failing and many reasons for those failures. But one of the main reasons businesses fail in the growth phase is due to unplanned rapid growth.

My clients had a car-detailing business, and they were the best at what they did. They used environmentally friendly products, so they charged a little more, and they serviced their customers' cars from a shop they rented. As time went by, they realized that more and more people were using their services because of the environmentally friendly products. As demand rose, so did their rent. Instead of renegotiating their lease with the landlord or looking for a new shop to rent, they decided to obtain a loan and buy their own shop.

Within a few months of buying their shop, they decided they wanted to reach customers outside their local community and implemented mobile car-detailing services. They had to drive to the customer's location, so they charged more on top of their already high prices. For the mobile car-detailing service, they needed to hire employees. Without running the numbers, they hired fifteen employees to drive to customer locations and provide the service. My clients failed to realize that some markets are just not profitable. You can spend time, energy, and lots of money reaching them, but some markets are not willing to pay top dollar for your service.

Within eight months of buying a new shop and hiring fifteen employees, they came to the realization that they could no longer pay all their expenses and still stay in business. They lost the new shop and were forced to start over again.

Why waste so much of your time and money reaching a customer base that doesn't have the need or the means to buy your product or service? It would have made much more sense for my clients to stay small and serve the customers who were happy and willing to pay for their services.

Growing a business you have nurtured from the beginning can be exciting. However, just because you have succeeded in entering the growth phase does not mean your business will sustain the growth. It is important to be aware of the common mistakes that can occur during the growth phase and hinder your growth. Here are the three most common mistakes I see business owners make while growing their company and ways to overcome them:

1. **Not defining the company's mission, vision, and values**
   It sounds simple, but having a clearly defined mission, vision, and set of values can help achieve alignment in your company.

   - The mission statement is the core of your company's purpose: what the company does, and what the desired outcome is.

   - The vision of the company should keep you and your employees motivated. It is the business owner's role to create the vision of where the company is going and share that vision with the employees to make sure everyone understands where the company is headed.

- Values are the principles and behaviors that describe how the company does business and what impression you want your customers and clients to have.

2. Not understanding the roles and responsibilities of the business owner
Too many business owners think their job is to make all the decisions and be at the center of everything. The fact is that too many business owners find themselves working "in the business" rather than "on the business." You need to understand how your roles and responsibilities change during the various stages of growth and how your behavior affects the company's growth. It is very important for the business owner to delegate, communicate effectively, and plan ahead so he or she doesn't become the obstacle to the growth of the company.

3. Relying on luck
Some companies are in the right place at the right time and experience growth because the economy was growing, the owner had good networks, and business came his way without having to do much. If you are going to keep your business moving up the growth curve, you need to be prepared for a market change and have a growth strategy that targets various customers and clients. You need to plan for the future and develop the infrastructure to support growth.

PART THREE

ESTABLISHED PHASE

CHAPTER SEVEN

HOW DO WE STAY COMPETITIVE?

"I've missed more than 9,000 shots in my career.
I've lost almost 300 games. Twenty-six times I've
been trusted to take the game-winning shot and
missed. I've failed over and over and over again
in my life, and that is why I succeed."
– Michael Jordan

A business goes through stages of development similar to the human cycle of life. Parenting strategies that work for your toddler cannot be applied to your teenager. The same goes for your business. It will face different cycles throughout its life. What you focus on today will change and require different approaches to maintain success. This brings us to the established phase of your business.

WHAT IS ESTABLISHED?

There are many ways to define an established business, but the one that really resonates is when your business has matured into a thriving company with a place in the market and loyal customers or clients. Sales growth is not explosive, but manageable, and business life has become more routine. An established business will be focused on improvement and productivity.

To compete in an established market, you will need better business practices along with automation and outsourcing to improve productivity.

I have found that when business owners reach this phase, the planning is about making decisions today based on your assessment of likely future events. It is also about trying to minimize risks.

The number one question business owners ask in the established or third phase of the business lifecycle is:

HOW DO WE STAY COMPETITIVE?

Question that should be asked: How do we make the most of our established position?

The longer you have been in a business sector or market, the more knowledgeable you will be. To remain successful in business, you must continually innovate. Keeping your products or services fresh and staying one step ahead of the competition is the key to sustaining your company's success. As an established business that wants to make the most of its strong position in the marketplace, focus on the following:

Stay in constant communication with your customers and clients
In the digital age, it's never been easier to create a sense of community with your customers and clients. Whether it is social media, e-newsletters or direct contact via customer events at the office, building on your existing relationship is a great way to retain customers and clients, as well as attract new ones.

Focus on what makes you different

New competition will pop up from time to time within your industry, and there will be pressure to offer what your competition is offering. Stay true to your products and services, as you know what these are, and what your customers like and will buy.

Know your competitors

You cannot stay one step ahead of the competition if you don't know whom you're competing with. Do some market research to find out who your competitors are, what they are selling, and how they message their brand. Not only will this help you identify areas in which you can compete, but it will also give you a platform for differentiating your brand.

Innovate your products and services on your own terms

Any good business is analytical about what it is selling and will always strive to provide better products and services. Work hard to continue improving your products and services, and staying ahead of the game.

Form a partnership

If you do not have the funds to expand your products or services, consider forming a strategic partnership with a noncompetitive business in your market. Not only will you have access to a completely new database of buyers, you can also share things such as marketing, advertising, product development, sales, and branding.

Continue building strong industry relationships with key partners

As an established business, you'll already have a network of suppliers, manufacturers, producers, and other relationships. These strong industry relationships put you in a position of strength moving forward. Make sure you nurture them.

Question that you don't know to ask: How do I stay focused?

You may have heard about business plans and paid no attention. After all, who has time to sit and write one?

Take another look at the concept of a business plan. What is a business plan? In its simplest form, a business plan is a guide, a road map for your business that outlines goals and details how you plan to achieve those goals.

Why should you devise a business plan? Here are some very important reasons for you to consider using a business plan:

To map the future

A business plan is a vital tool to help you manage your business more effectively. By committing your thoughts to paper, you can understand your business better and set specific courses of action needed to improve your business. A plan can detail alternative future scenarios, set specific objectives and goals, and include the resources required to achieve these goals.

To support growth and secure funding

Most businesses face investment decisions during the course of their lifetime. Often you can't fund these opportunities on your own and must seek funding elsewhere. Any investor who is interested in funding your business must have an excellent understanding of where the company is planning to go and what the company plans to do with the funding. Therefore, when seeking investment for your business, it is important to clearly describe the opportunity for potential investors. A well-written business plan can help you convey to the investor your company's future ability to generate sufficient cash flow to meet debt obligation, while enabling the business to operate effectively.

To develop and communicate a course of action

A business plan helps a company assess future opportunities and commit to a particular course of action. The plan can assign milestones to specific individuals and, ultimately, help management monitor progress.

To help manage cash flow

Careful management of cash flow is a fundamental requirement for all businesses. The reason is quite simple: many businesses fail, not because they are not profitable, but because they cannot pay their debts when due.

To support a strategic exit

Finally, at some point, you will decide it is time to exit your company. If you consider your likely exit strategy in advance, the plan will help you direct present-day decisions. You can make investment decisions now while keeping one eye on the future via a well-thought-out business plan.

KEY SECTIONS OF A BUSINESS PLAN

Some business plans will run four or five pages, while others will be forty-plus pages. The complexity of the business and details necessary to present a thorough picture of the business will define the appropriate length of your business plan. Regardless of the length of the plan, the same key elements need to be included:

Executive Summary

The executive summary provides an overview of the rest of the business plan. It is often considered the most crucial part of the plan because it is the first section your readers see and is designed to capture their attention. The executive summary should include:

- The overall objective of the business; what makes the business unique or distinctive
- The experience of the management team
- The target audience
- Future aspirations
- How the business will operate
- The current competition in the market
- Costs and financial projections

Company Description or Business Overview

This section is used to explain your vision and goals for the business venture in practical terms. The who, what, where, and why of the business should fall into place, and readers should have a clear understanding of how the company will function. Details that prospective investors will likely want to see are:

- The legal structure of the business
- Formation of the business
- Type of business

- Potential for profitability
- Geographical location of the business
- Means of doing business
- Resources required

Products or Services

This section describes the products sold or services offered. Explain the significant benefits of your products or services and how they provide something other than that which is currently available.

Market Information

Market information describes the larger picture of the industry in which your business will compete. This sets a framework so that investors will see what piece of this market you will be able to capture and from where you will build your customer base. It also provides you, the business owner, with an opportunity to carefully research and evaluate the industry to better determine how you can make an impact. Market information must be timely, accurate, and easy to understand. Furthermore, you should present:

- An overview of the market
- Trends and changes in the market
- Niche markets and segments within the larger market
- Your target audience
- The needs of your target audience
- How you will impact those needs
- How you anticipate the market will change over the next five years

Competitive Analysis

Business is competitive by nature, and to succeed it is vital that you research, understand, and evaluate your competition. The strengths, weaknesses, and details of the most direct and indirect competition should be included in this section of your business plan.

Management and Ownership

This section features short biographies of the key personnel involved in forming and running the business. Explaining who is behind the company and what each person brings to the table is of great interest to any potential investor.

Financial Plan

From startup costs to the day-to-day operational budget, a solid financial plan should be outlined within the overall business plan. The financial section should outline:

- How much money is necessary to start the business
- How much money will be needed over the next two to five years
- How funds will be used
- A timeline of when you will need funding

You may purchase a business plan template by going to www.BaglaLaw.com/essentials

KEY POINTS:

▶ As lifecycles of humans change, so do the lifecycles for your business. Knowing how to develop strategies for the different cycles is critical to the success of your business.

▶ To remain in the established phase as a key player, you should consider creating strategic partnerships with noncompetitive businesses.

▶ A business plan is your road map to keep you on track and help prepare your business for exit.

CHAPTER EIGHT

WHAT'S NEXT FOR MY BUSINESS?

Companies in the established phase must continually evolve to stay relevant, innovative and competitive. Choosing the right approach to adapt and grow is difficult. As a result, many companies find a model and stick with it, even if it is not effective.

I have watched a handful of my clients in the established phase evolve by buying out their competition or merging with strategic partners, which allows them to retain their competitive edge. The second most frequently asked question I hear from business owners in the established phase is:

WHAT'S NEXT FOR MY BUSINESS?

Question that should be asked: How do I expand to other markets?

At this stage, I'm assuming you have established your business within your industry and now are looking to expand your market. Just because you are a small business does not mean you should not be thinking big. Business owners usually start doing business in their own state and then expand to other states. Sometimes it may make sense for the business owner to be ambitious and consider expanding globally. Reasons for expanding globally include increased sales, improved profits, and increased innovation, to list only a few.

Whether you are expanding nationwide or globally, you should do your research first and gain a deep understanding of the targeted markets, the competition, market trends in the areas you're targeting, and the requirements to successfully launch and drive your business into those markets.

Before taking action and expanding into new territory, it is critical to understand what the full impact on your business will be. Here are some questions you should consider before entering the nationwide or international business world:

- Will the product or service sell well in the targeted market? The good news is that most American products and services are embraced both nationally and overseas.

- Is your target market familiar with your product or service? If not, be prepared to invest a lot of time and money in consumer education. On the flip side, if you are the first one to introduce a new and exciting concept, the product then becomes synonymous with your company name.

- Do you feel comfortable in that state or country? Since you might have to live there temporarily to operate the business in its early stages, you will need a working knowledge of the way business is done in that state or country.

Here are additional things to research:

- Prepare a market segmentation analysis to determine if your product or service will sell in that market.

- Prepare a product analysis to see if there is a demand that is not satisfied by the local businesses.

- Perform an analysis against competition.

- Consider how big the market is and how long it will take you to capture your targeted sales.

Question that you don't know to ask: How do I prepare to expand in other markets?

As a business owner who wants to take your business to the next level, it pays to do your homework. Start early and strategize as to where you want to take your business; not every business is suited for such expansion. Here are some important factors to consider and put into motion:

Develop a strategy and business plan

Each market has its own nuances due to economic, cultural, governmental, and market conditions. It is important to develop a strategy and business plan that drives success in the new markets while remaining integrated with the overall company strategy and objectives.

Establish a strong team

Many companies try to launch their expansion with a team put together rapidly from scratch. This is time-consuming, risky, and slows time to market. Using proven senior interim team members allows the company to hit the ground running, while the company hires the right senior management team to take over the new markets. Remember – hire slow and fire fast.

Establish a go-to-market strategy

This is important, as effective selling and marketing of your products or services requires a comprehensive strategy that addresses the following:

- Sales delivery
- Branding
- Marketing
- Pricing

Legal readiness

Some states and countries are known for being highly litigious, so it is critical to put strong legal processes in place to minimize risk. Also, government agencies have strict requirements that necessitate legal documentation be in place prior to operating within the state or country. Being proactive does require money upfront, but this more than offsets downstream risks and liabilities. Here are some proactive actions to consider:

- Create localized commercial agreements addressing dispute resolution.
- Review industry-specific regulations to ensure that compliance and certifications are obtained if needed.
- Maintain corporate records and governance.

Tax and financial readiness

The proper tax and financial infrastructures need to be set up early on to ensure that you can take full advantage of the tax benefits available to your business. Here are some actions to take:

- Set up accounting and payroll.
- Establish local banking relationships.
- Develop a risk-management plan with your CPA.

The number one advantage you can give your business is hiring professionals, such as business attorneys and certified public accountants, to help you succeed. You cannot and should not do everything yourself.

KEY POINTS:

▶ Going nationwide or international is very different from doing business in your state. Do your homework before you go down this road.

▶ Spend time conducting research on the different states or countries you may want to expand in, as every state and country has its own rules and regulations.

▶ Do not do this alone. Align yourself with professionals who have experience expanding into other states and countries.

CHAPTER NINE

HOW DO WE RETAIN OUR PEOPLE?

Hiring employees is just a start to creating a strong workforce. Next, you have to keep them. Studies have shown time and again that high employee turnover costs business owners in time, productivity and, most importantly, money. While it's not easy to find good employees that you can rely on, it's even more difficult keeping them motivated and inspired to work hard. Many jobs become routine for employees who eventually seek greener pastures elsewhere.

In the established phase, employee turnover should not be as high as it might have been in earlier stages. By now you should have created a company culture where employees want to work and stay. The third most frequently asked question in the established phase is:

HOW DO WE RETAIN OUR PEOPLE?

Question that should be asked: What incentives can I provide for my people?

According to strategic planning consultant Leigh Branham, author of *The 7 Hidden Reasons Employees Leave*, 88 percent of employees leave their jobs for reasons other than pay. However, 70 percent of managers think employees leave mainly for pay-related reasons. Branham's seven reasons employees leave a company are:

1. Employees feel the job or workplace is not what they expected.
2. There is a mismatch between the job and person.
3. There is too little coaching and feedback.
4. There are too few growth and advancement opportunities.
5. Employees feel devalued and unrecognized.
6. Employees feel stress from overwork and have a work/life imbalance.
7. There is a loss of trust and confidence in senior leaders.

After you put in the time, effort, and investment to hire the best employees possible, your goal should be to retain that talent. Salary, retirement plans, and vacations benefits are high on the list of why employees take the job, but they are not enough to keep them in your employ for the long haul. Job satisfaction will increase your employee retention rate.

Here are a few strategies you can use to retain your top talent:

Create an environment that makes your employees feel like an asset to your company

Don't make them feel like overhead. Allow them to feel secure in their job and know what their contributions are to the company. Get their input about your company, and encourage goal setting so they feel a sense of accomplishment once the goals are achieved.

Make expectations and goals of the company clear

Be sure you have job descriptions, so your employees know what is required of them. If changes need to be made, don't expect them to pick that up by osmosis. You must communicate directly and clearly. Good employees want to please you, but they need to know what they must do to make that happen.

Provide opportunities to grow and learn, and let your employees know there is room for advancement in your company

Provide tuition for continuing education classes, which shows that you really care about providing opportunities for advancement. Give them challenging and stimulating work. Let them know what career-development plans you have for them and what opportunities are available for them to grow with the company.

Recognize and reward good work

Monetary bonuses are always nice, but recognition of a job well done goes a long way toward creating goodwill and loyalty. Recognition needs to be specific. What's more, don't hesitate to mention projects employees are working on so they know you are engaged with what they are doing. In order to retain talent, you must make them feel appreciated, respected, and worthwhile. They need to feel that their contributions to the company are important.

Provide flexible schedules

Many businesses are allowing employees to work alternative schedules that do not adhere to the traditional 9 to 5 workday. This might include part-time schedules or even job sharing, where two people share one full-time position.

Administer performance reviews

Conduct regularly scheduled performance reviews that include positive feedback and let employees know what is expected of them.

Other Motivators
- Allow employees to enhance, improve, and decorate their own workspace.

- Provide a means of socialization through lunchtime or after-hours activities.

- Have an open-door policy, which encourages employees to ask questions or make recommendations.

- Make donations to charities selected by the employees on behalf of the company.

I have seen business owners lose their top people to customers or clients, or to the competition. This happens more often than you think. Without putting in safeguards for your business, such as having a non-solicitation clause in your employee contract, you have just lost the money invested in that employee, often as much or more than $100,000. As mentioned above, top employees are not created overnight: you put in money, time, and effort to train them. Losing them could be disastrous for your company. Now you need to look for someone else and put money, time, and effort into training this new person. All the while, you are losing money from projects your top employee could have been working on.

Question that you don't know to ask: What type of internal policies can I create to retain my top talent?

Good retention starts from the time you hire employees to the time they leave your company. At this stage of your company, you should have certain internal policies and procedures set, so you don't have to re-create the wheel every time you need to hire someone. Having these policies in place can save you a lot of money and time. Here are some key strategies you can use to create your internal retention policies:

Recruitment and hiring

It is worth spending time and effort on recruiting. When there is a good match between employees and your company, retention is less likely to be an issue.

Orientation and onboarding

Have good practices in place when hiring employees, so they fit right in and get to work right away. Treating employees right in the critical early stages of employment has proved to enhance retention.

Training and development

Training and development are key factors in helping employees grow with your company.

Performance evaluations

When employees know what they are doing well and where they need to improve, both they and your company benefit.

Pay and benefits

While today many employees tend to rate factors such as career development higher than pay, good pay and benefits still count, and show that you are vested in them.

Internal communications

Effective communication can help ensure that employees want to stay with your company. Employees need to know and be reminded on a regular basis how the company is performing and what they can do to help.

Termination and outplacement

Employees who leave on good terms are much more likely to recommend your company and, in doing so, help attract and retain future employees.

Other ways to incentivize employees can include a variety of possible arrangements, including stock options, bonuses and profit-sharing plans.

Stock Option Plan

Stock option plans are typically structured so that an employee must be employed by the company for a certain amount of time before he or she is able to exercise the option. Stock option plans still remain a valuable part of a long-term incentive package for employees who are expected to remain with the company for many years.

Bonuses

A monetary bonus can certainly serve as an incentive. However, it can also set a standard that may be hard to follow. Once word spreads that an employee received a monetary bonus, others will anticipate the same for their good work. Therefore, unless the bonus is part of an employment agreement, you need to establish a policy that details the expectations of an employee before he or she will be eligible to receive such a bonus. Besides cash bonuses, other types of incentive bonuses include gifts, extra vacation time, or extra personal days.

Profit-Sharing Plan

If a company is doing well, sharing profits with employees serves as a very strong incentive. Such plans will need to be carefully designed and spelled out with the assistance of professionals.

Retirement Plans

Many companies offer 401(k) plans, which are retirement plans for long-term employee savings. Again, this type of plan should be created with the assistance of professionals.

Smaller businesses that are not yet seeing significant profits can provide incentives that might include flexible schedules, telecommuting, or additional vacation days.

The types of incentives you offer will depend largely on:

- The size of your business and number of employees
- The structure of your business
- The profitability of your business
- The level of experience and base salaries of the employees
- The economic climate

KEY POINTS:

▶ Knowing why employees leave their job can be advantageous to your business. Avoid doing whatever prompts them to go elsewhere.

▶ Safeguard your business from sudden loss of a top employee by having the correctly worded employee contracts with your top people.

▶ Put retention policies in place. These can dramatically reduce the employee turnover rate.

A STORY OF CAUTION FOR ESTABLISHED COMPANIES

I was hired by an IT computer company that had just celebrated 10 years in business. My client grew this business from the ground up by hiring ambitious people. My client taught these employees all about IT work and invested in additional training. My client values his employees, so pays top dollar to show his appreciation.

My client shared with me that he had a very talented employee who had been with the company for 10 years. My client had invested money, resources, and training in this employee. Then, without any warning, the employee gave his two weeks' notice and left the company. This sudden departure of a top employee cost my client $100,000 that year as my client tried to replace the talent he had lost.

In order to minimize this type of loss in the future, I ensured that he signed contracts with each employee. The contract stipulated that if a customer wanted to hire any of the company's employees, that customer would pay for the loss of revenue until my client found and replaced the employee.

As a business owner, preparation is key, and being aware of some of the reasons that lead to loss of key employees is critical. We've already discussed some of the reasons employees leave. Here are some of the mistakes my clients have shared with me, and ways to avoid them:

Failure to provide vision
Most employees do not get out of bed each morning trying to hit a profit number. They get out of bed to be a part of your company's

vision and work toward achieving it. Successful business owners sell their employees on a vision of the future.

Failure to provide empathy

Generally speaking, in today's workforce there is very little loyalty on either side. There is, however, a simple solution for this problem—take the time to listen to your employees. The employee should leave the conversation believing you will take action on what was discussed. By leaving your door open to employee concerns and suggestions, you encourage them to feel they have a stake in the company; that you consider them important and care enough to listen.

Failure to provide stimulating projects

Top talent is not driven by money or power. They are driven by the opportunity to be a part of something that will make a difference and that they are passionate about.

Failure to provide guidance for career development

Almost every employee wants to have a discussion with you about his or her future, and most business owners never engage with their employees about where they want their career to take them. Having that conversation with your top talent can provide a huge opportunity for you and your company. If your best employees know there is a path for them going forward, they will be more likely to hang around.

PART FOUR
EXIT PHASE

CHAPTER TEN

HOW DO I RETIRE?

"Disciplining yourself to do what you know is right
and important, although difficult, is the high road
to pride, self-esteem, and personal satisfaction."
– Margaret Thatcher

Ask most business owners about their exit strategy, and you are likely to get a blank stare. That's because the last thing on their minds is when and how they will leave their business. Their focus is on being in the game or competing in their industry. Most owners understand the logic of planning for an exit, but typically put it off to some unknown point in the future.

This brings us to the fourth and final phase of your business's Legal Lifecycle, the exit phase.

WHAT IS AN EXIT?

Investopedia defines exit as, "An entrepreneur's strategic plan to sell his or her investment in a company he or she founded. An exit strategy gives a business owner a way to reduce or eliminate his or her stake in the business and, if the business is successful, make a substantial profit. If the business is not successful, an exit strategy enables the entrepreneur to limit losses."

Just as you needed a plan to get into business, you'll need a plan to get out of it. Selling or otherwise disposing of a business requires some forethought, strategizing, and careful implementation. In some ways, it is more complicated than starting a business. For instance, while there is really only one way to start a company, there are at three primary methods for business owners to leave the business they founded. These methods are: selling, merging, or closing your business.

The number one question I am asked by business owners in the exit phase is:

HOW DO I RETIRE?

Question that should be asked: What is my most likely option for exit from my business?

Deciding to sell the business you have worked so hard to grow is rarely an easy decision. Most business owners have the majority of their wealth in their illiquid, privately held business. In addition, most owners and their companies have a rather risky and unhealthy co-dependency. In other words, the business owner depends on the company for income, perks, and a sense of fulfillment. The company, in turn, is dependent upon the owner for strategic, operational, and financial decisions, and, in most cases, personal guarantees on company liabilities.

If business owners think about who might own the business after them, it can help to alleviate some of this co-dependency. In most cases, the potential buyer will evaluate the future value of a company based on the business's strength and its ability to perform without the current owner. If the success of the business is highly dependent on that owner, the value and future of the business is at risk and may affect a successful transition. For example:

- Are the sales and customer relationships dependent solely on the owner for success?

- Does the owner make all critical strategic and operational decisions alone, or is there a strong management team in place?

A planned exit strategy will help reduce owner dependency and perhaps further empower a management team that can either take over ownership or help a new owner continue to run the company successfully.

Most business owners are not aware that a number of options are available for a customized exit. These options include:

- Private sale
- Management buyout
- Co-owner buyout
- An employee stock ownership plan
- Gifting the business to family members

There are three ways to exit your business. Let's begin with the first method: exiting your business by selling your business. Selling your business may be preferable to owning if:

- You are ready to retire and have no heirs to continue the company.
- Partners who own the business decide to dissolve their partnership.
- One of the owners dies or becomes disabled and is unable to participate in the business.
- You or another owner get divorced and need cash for a settlement.
- You want to do something more challenging, more fun, and less stressful.
- You do not have enough working capital to keep the business going.
- The company needs new skills, a new approach, or resources you cannot provide.

If you are aware of the factors that indicate that selling your business is a good idea, you can time the sale to take advantage of high prices. Usually, you will get the most for your company when sales are climbing and profits are strong. If you have a history of solid performances, by all means sell the company before trouble strikes. Other factors that may affect the timing of a sale are availability of bank financing, interest rate trends, changes in tax law, and the general economic climate.

You can sell your business yourself, but many business owners hire a business attorney and a professional business broker to handle the job. Your business attorney will advise you on the relevant legal, tax, and preparation considerations, and your business broker protects your anonymity and confidentiality. If you are advertising your business for sale and showing it to prospects, it compromises your ability to continue leading the company. Your business broker can be the face for your business, screening prospects and keeping the identity of your business secret from all but qualified buyers.

Most business buyers are individuals like you who want to become small-business owners. But sometimes you can transfer ownership of your business to another business in a merger or acquisition. As a rule, businesses have deeper pockets and borrowing power than individuals, and they may be willing to pay more than individuals. Businesses also tend to be more savvy buyers than individuals, increasing the changes that your business will survive, albeit perhaps as a division or subsidiary of another company. So, how do you prepare your business for a merger or acquisition?

Merging your business with another business may be preferable if:

- Your company has a strong financial history.
- Your company's technology and intellectual property are protected.
- Customer sales and loyalty are strong.
- Your employees are willing to continue with the new owners.
- Your company is a proper fit for the buyer.

The best candidate for a merger is a company that sees your business as a strategic fit. If you have something it wants, such as a unique product or distribution channel, the purchaser may be willing to pay a premium price.

Sometimes, the best thing to do is simply sell your inventory and fixtures, pay your creditors and employees, close your doors, and walk away.

Closing your company may be the best option if:

- Your business is failing.
- Your business is not valuable enough for anyone to want to acquire it.

- Your business is the type of business that is unlikely to be valuable without you personally operating it.

Question that you don't know to ask: What should I know before exiting my business?

Selling your business is never an easy or simple process. It is exactly that: a process. Ideally, an exit strategy is planned at the outset of a business. However, because businesses are so fluid, it can be difficult to know what the final version of the business will look like. For a mature company, the sooner a plan is put into place, the better prepared an owner will be when an exit is available, both personally and professionally.

The planning starts with determining your personal and business goals, and then assessing your mental and financial readiness. After that you need to identify the exit options most aligned with your goals.

When helping clients prepare for their exit, I have found that having discussions on six key things tend to maximize their chances of success:

1. Potential does not sell
Sometimes business owners believe they have a potential gold mine and expect a high selling price based on perceived potential alone. This is not how it works. Buyers want to acquire something that is already successful and a proven business.

2. Buyers are interested in profits, not revenue
Revenue sounds good. But when it comes down to it, the only number that matters is the profit your business makes.

3. Honest financials

The number one document all buyers look at is the business financials—and verifiable proof of those financials. For instance, be prepared to show invoices and bank deposits reflecting your numbers.

4. Past successes are not recent successes

The previous success of a business is largely irrelevant at the time of sale, especially if your business has been struggling lately. Buyers are interested in recent performance, usually the last 12 months, and future sustainability. Buyers are not interested in fixing and recovering your business (unless it's Marcus Lemonis of CNBC's *The Profit*), especially if you are expecting them to pay a premium. However, make sure you show the buyer previous years if the business has been growing steadily. Buyers love to see growing revenue and profit figures, especially if you have already made future plans for the business that seem realistic based on past performance.

5. Honesty is the best policy

The truth is always going to surface, so be upfront about everything from the beginning. Experienced buyers understand that every business has positives and negatives. There is no such thing as a perfect business. If you are honest and transparent from the start, there is less risk of a deal going sour because the buyer uncovered something during due diligence that wasn't presented accurately. Honesty is the best policy in all business transactions, and selling your business is no different.

6. Expect to answer a lot of questions

I'm sure you would not walk into a house and decide to buy it without first asking a lot of questions. The same is true of your business. Prospects will not buy a business without first asking a lot of questions, and you need to be prepared to answer them, regardless of how simple or complex they may be. Never judge buyers; you never know whom you are dealing with or the buying power they possess.

KEY POINTS:

▶ Retiring from your business is a process and not an event. Plan early, as you never know when someone might be interested in buying your company.

▶ There are many options available that will allow for your retirement. Speak to professionals, and understand what option would be best for you.

▶ Preparing for an exit should be part of the planning process for your business. An exit strategy should be put together sooner rather than later. This will help guide you in the right direction.

CHAPTER ELEVEN

Whom Do I Sell My Business To?

Selling your business is a complex venture. You may need to enlist a business broker, an accountant, and a business attorney as you proceed to sell your business. Depending on the level of your connection and involvement in your business, you do not want to sell to just anyone.

When my clients get to this stage and are ready for sale, the number two question I am asked is:

Whom do I sell my business to?

Question that should be asked: How can I make my business ready for sale to a potential buyer?

To answer this question, you need to consider the reason for the sale so you can explain it to buyers. This is one of the first questions a potential buyer will ask. In my experience, business owners commonly sell their business for any of the following reasons:

- Retirement
- Partnership disputes
- Illness and death
- Being overworked

- Boredom
- Not making money

Most of the reasons listed are a result of business owners' failure to develop an exit plan for their business, which is a huge mistake. As mentioned, you should develop an exit plan for your business from the very beginning. Having an exit plan will help you keep the business going in the right direction by constantly aligning with your long-term goals. In your exit plan, you may want to list the following four steps that can help prepare your business for potential sale. Work toward them constantly, so when the time is right, you are able to sell your business on your terms.

1. Finding buyers

One thing business owners fail to think about is finding buyers for their business. Most owners just assume someone will want to buy their business. Keeping a list of potential buyers is a critical piece of your exit plan. You should also keep a list of competitors who may be interested in acquiring your business when the time is right.

2. A good growth pattern

Having a business that has shown good growth patterns is what you are aiming for and what buyers will want to see. Steady and predictable financial growth is the goal. You may have some dips in your growth patterns here and there, but as long as they can be explained, you will be fine. What a buyer does not want to see is erratic swings in your growth.

3. Standard operating procedures

If you do not have a written set of detailed standard operating procedures, you need to develop them right away. Build your business to the point where, if you get hit by a bus and killed, your business will move forward without any disruption. You really want to detail everything in your standard procedures, including but not limited to:

- Executive strategy, including the vision, mission, core values, and management practices
- Marketing plan, including the tools used to attract prospects to your company
- Sales plan and procedures, including what tools and processes your business uses to convert prospects to customers
- Operating procedures, including detailed processes of how your business works day in and day out

4. Good bookkeeping

No company gets acquired without a good set of books. Business owners struggle with accounting and bookkeeping, so you should find a good bookkeeping service to help you keep solid records from the start. That will prove vital to your growth and exit.

Question that you don't know to ask: What are the most common mistakes I can make while selling my business?

You need to know what could cause your exit to go wrong and how to avoid that. Here are some of the most common mistakes business owners make while selling their business:

1. Rushing the sale

Selling your business should in theory be an objective decision, though in reality it is often very emotional. Sometimes there can be a desire just to get out of it, which could lead to problems, such as selling it to the wrong buyer—who now does not want the business—or selling it for a lot less than your company is worth. The more time, planning, and strategy you put into the sale of your business, the better off you will be.

2. Not considering what is actually for sale

Remember that your business is made up of lots of different assets, which can be divided. You can sell some assets and retain others. Businesses almost always have a number of intangible assets, such as intellectual property and goodwill, that can be retained or added to the price of your business when you sell. Consider speaking to a business attorney to determine which assets are sellable and which are not.

3. Not doing due diligence

Due diligence is really just checking your facts. If you are selling your business, you need to check on whether the buyer has or can get the required financing, and if the buyer has experience in running a business.

4. Problems with handover

Sometimes business sales go wrong on practical and simple matters when the business is handed over to the buyer. The details and timing of the handover should all be written in your purchase agreement or sales contract, which should be prepared by your business attorney to ensure all details are included. You should also consider:

- Introducing the buyer to your most important clients
- Introducing the buyer to your most important suppliers
- Introducing the buyer to all of your employees

- Making sure you hand over all keys and security devices
- Transferring all utilities into the name of the buyer

5. Not considering your legal obligations

There are a number of legal obligations you need to take into consideration, such as:

- Do your business licenses, if any, need to be canceled, or can they be transferred to the buyer?
- What is going to happen to your trademarks?
- Have you fulfilled all your final tax obligations?
- Do you need to cancel or transfer your lease?
- Do you need to transfer any contracts to the buyer?
- Do you need to cut final paychecks to employees?

KEY POINTS:

▶ Understand why you are selling your business because any potential buyer will want to know.

▶ Prepare to sell your business by following the four steps in helping you get ready for sale—finding buyers, establishing a good growth pattern, standardizing operating procedures, and hiring/maintaining good bookkeeping.

▶ Know the common mistakes you can make while selling your business, so you can avoid making them.

CHAPTER TWELVE

WHAT RISKS DO I FACE BEFORE I EXIT?

Since selling a business is a complex process, there are many obvious pitfalls and mistakes you can make. Some of these mistakes can cost you a lot, but the good news is that the majority of them are pretty easy to avoid with some advance planning.

The third most frequently asked question I get from business owners in the exit phase is:

WHAT RISKS DO I FACE BEFORE I EXIT?

Question that should be asked: How do I minimize the risk in my exit strategy?

As a business owner, you have worked hard all your life to get to the point where you are now ready to sell your business and reap the benefits, which can be both overwhelming and emotional. The best strategy is always taking it step-by-step, allowing yourself to get comfortable with the idea of selling and minimizing the risk of missing important steps.

Here is a checklist I have put together over the years, which has helped clients stay on track and minimized their risk while they prepare to exit their company:

Your exit team

Business Attorney – Engage a business attorney, not a generalist, to prepare the relevant documents for the sale of your company.

Business Broker – Engage a business broker who has experience in your field of work.

Certified Public Accountant – Engage a certified public accountant who can prepare your financials for sale and advise you on your best possible tax situation.

Hitting the projections

Do not let the exit process distract you from your most important job, which is conducting business as usual and hitting or exceeding your financial projections.

Corporate structure

Review your company minutes, and all board and shareholder meetings to ensure you are able to exit your company legally. Discuss the ownership structure of your company with your exit team to ensure optimum tax treatment in either a share or an asset sale.

Intellectual property, employment and contractor agreements

Make sure your company owns the assets of the business and that all things that have created goodwill for your company are protected through some sort of trademark. Review every employee and contractor agreements to ensure you are able to sell your company without difficulties.

Tax review

Review tax liabilities with your certified public accountant and how best to minimize them. Have on hand at least five years' worth of financial history and at least three years' worth of projections.

Question that you don't know to ask: What are the most common mistakes you can make while selling your business?

Most business owners do not expect the exit from their company to be easy, but many are surprised by how difficult it can be to sell their business for a good price in a reasonable time frame. The majority of challenges business owners experience could be avoided easily with a little information upfront about the pitfalls. While this list is by no means exhaustive, here are some of the most common mistakes I have seen business owners make over the years:

Slowing of business

Many business owners seem to check out once they list their business for sale. This is one of the worst things you can do. This attitude will result in revenue slump because you took your foot off the gas, and the business will start tanking. When potential buyers find a downward trend in revenue, they will be much less open to paying the asking price. Continue working on your business as if you were not selling it.

Insufficient preparation

Lack of preparation is by far the most common mistake business owners make. Just like you would spruce up your house before hanging a "For Sale" sign in the front yard, it is important to address several key aspects of your business before listing it for sale. Financial documentation, sustainable profitability, lease issues, staffing problems, and other concerns will not only impact salability, but also the price your business will command.

Overvaluing

Far too many business owners overvalue their business and think they will get top dollar for it simply because they believe that is the worth of their business. In the real world, valuation is based on quantifiable criteria, not the owner's personal estimation of worth. To avoid this mistake, get an objective third-party valuation early in the process. Once you have identified an appropriate valuation for your business, address the issues that could increase value.

Unwillingness to leverage professionals

You are an expert at running your business, not selling it. Yet many business owners are averse to hiring a business broker to facilitate the sale of their business. You probably think that by not hiring a business broker you are saving at least 10 percent, but in reality, business brokers are capable of adding at least 10 percent to 15 percent to the sale price. In certain circumstances a "for sale by owner" approach makes sense, but most business owners are better off hiring a broker to handle important tasks like preparation, showing the business to potential buyers, marketing, and negotiation. Likewise, you should also leverage the expertise of other professionals, such as business attorneys, accountants, and financial consultants. It takes a team to prepare, protect, and sell your business, so consider using these professionals.

Misrepresentation

As a business owner selling your business, you want to portray your company in the best possible light. However, there is a big difference between representing your business in the best light and misrepresenting your business to prospective buyers. At some point during the selling process, you will be tempted to exaggerate numbers, distort projections, or even cover up problems. Misrepresentation sends up red flags when prospects review the actual financials or become the basis for legal action after the sale. Talk to your business attorney about everything before passing the information on to the buyer.

Failure to address transition issues

Many business owners are so focused on selling their business that they completely neglect the transition process that will occur after closing. Some buyers will insist that you remain for a few months to assist with the transition or training, while others prefer a clean break. Either way is fine, as long as the buyer and you have discussed the transition and reached a mutually acceptable arrangement during negotiations.

KEY POINTS:

▶ Preparing is the best strategy to minimize risk in selling your business.

▶ Use professionals to prepare your business for sale.

▶ Use checklists to help you stay on track and to avoid common pitfalls.

Speaking of checklists, I've developed an Exit Strategy checklist that lists the critical steps to take in order to get the most value from your business. Go to www.BaglaLaw.com/GLYexit

A STORY OF CAUTION FOR EXITING COMPANIES

I used to get together with one client every year, and each time I would ask her, "Bella, have you told your guys that you want them to buy the business?" She had a plan to eventually sell her dog pampering business to her senior employees, but she had yet to inform them of this fact. "I'm not ready yet," she would say.

Then we would go another year, and the same thing would happen: "I'm not ready yet." Finally, she called one day and said, "I want to be out of here in six months."

"Bella," I asked, "have you talked to your guys yet?"

"No," she said.

Bella finally approached the two employees, who had been with her for twelve years. She told them, "I would like to retire in six months, and I'm willing to sell the business to you." Their immediate reaction? They thought the business was in trouble and that Bella was trying to push them under the bus. The sudden news of the sale was not received well. The two employees felt Bella had betrayed them, especially since they had worked for her for twelve years. As it happens, the two employees always wanted to buy Bella's company but did not have the money to do so. Six months was not enough time for them to get the money, and Bella could not find another buyer in time.

After twelve years of hard work, Bella had to close her doors and walk away from what could have been a lucrative payout. Instead, the business she built, her legacy, her retirement all disappeared.

Now, here is how this is supposed to work:

I had another client, a general contractor. He had started working on transferring his business about four years before I met him, and about ten years before he wanted to sell.

He chose two people who were already working in the company. They were young, they were paid well, and they were happy with what they were doing. "Look," he told them, "I'm going to be out of here in ten years. You're going to own the company if you want it. Here's what you need to do."

And he laid it out for them. Over that ten-year period, he got a chance to test their management capabilities. Were they able to run the business? This is especially important because when you sell a business internally, one thing is always true: your buyers are not going to have any money. In effect, you are going to have to be their bank.

That's a big risk. If they can't run the business, they will never be able to pay you what you're owed. Testing and developing their management skills before you pull the trigger is the best way to ensure that you get your money.

But here's the positive side: if you have to be the bank, it is better to be the bank for somebody you know.

In this case, my client got a chance to see the managers in action and see them run the company. He worked less and less and took more time off. For close to four years, he came into the office only a couple of days a week. For that four-year period, he got to enjoy the cash flow the business created with very little work on his part.

When it came time to sell, he pulled the trigger, and it was done. He walked away, and the business is still very successful. In fact, it's even more successful now than when he owned it.

CONCLUSION

Every business has a Legal Lifecycle: a startup phase, a growth phase, an established phase, and an exit phase. You, as a business owner, have the capacity to become successful by knowing what phase your business is in. After working with dozens of business owners, I discovered that the successful ones share some common traits:

- They know where they are in the Legal Lifecycle of their business.
- They create a business strategy and follow it. If necessary, they make adjustments to the business plan to stay on track.
- They have a financial road map and know at all times what their financial capacity is.
- They create business processes and understand the need to continuously improve them to become more efficient and productive.
- They search out a team of advisors because these people know what they don't know.

I hope this book was educational and inspirational. I applaud you business owners who wake up every day and work hard to do what you love. As an attorney and business owner, I too know the pain of hard work—as well as the joy of great rewards.

Here's to you – my fellow business owners.

GO LEGAL YOURSELF™ PRODUCTS

What is the most common mistake startups and fast-growth companies that are serious about winning in business make during the early stages of their Legal Lifecycle? Not having the RIGHT contracts, which are specialized to accommodate the current phase of the Legal Lifecycle of their business. Why do you think this is? Simply put, they don't know what they don't know. No one has offered them the complete specialized legal package relevant to where they are in business, plus a one-stop shop that includes access to an expert in the Legal Lifecycle, until now.

Go Legal Yourself™ offers two packages: the Startup Essentials Package and the Growth Essentials Package. Finally! Specialized packages that include everything a startup company and a company that's growing fast would need to run a business and protect its assets.

STARTUP ESSENTIALS PACKAGE:

- Corporation Formation Package
  - ✓ Articles of Incorporation
  - ✓ Bylaws
  - ✓ Sole Incorporator Resolution
  - ✓ Organizational Meeting Minutes
  - ✓ Founder's Stock Purchase Agreement
  - ✓ Form SS-4 to obtain Employer Identification Number (EIN)
  - ✓ Form 2553 to file as an S Corporation

- Promissory Note
- Services Agreement
- Independent Contractor Agreement
- Confidentiality Agreement
- Website Terms of Use
- Website Privacy Policy
- Website Disclaimer
- One Hour Legal Strategy Session with Kelly Bagla, Esq.

GROWTH ESSENTIALS PACKAGE:

Includes everything in the Startup Essentials Package, plus:

- Director Agreement
- Employee Handbook
- Employee Application Form
- Employee Agreement
- Invention Assignment Agreement
- Nondisclosure Agreement
- Shareholder Resolution Authorizing Stock
- Board of Director Resolution Authorizing Stock
- Shareholder Agreement
- Capital-Raising Business Plan Template
- Trademark Logo Assistance - Half Hour
- Three Hours Legal Strategy Session with Kelly Bagla, Esq.

To learn more about these two packages, visit www.BaglaLaw.com/essentials

OTHER BOOKS BY KELLY BAGLA, ESQ.

Kelly has an upcoming book called *Go Own Yourself!*

It is specifically written for women business owners who want to start with the basics: how to own yourself before you own your business. People want to do business with people who are confident in themselves. Confidence starts with Owning Yourself as a person, so you can Own your Business.

ABOUT THE AUTHOR

Kelly Bagla, Esq., the Queen of Business Law, is an experienced corporate attorney who practices in San Diego, California.

A multi-degree lawyer, she began her career with a Fortune 500 global biotechnology company in California, where she managed legal issues for domestic and international subsidiaries. She then joined the world's strongest global law firm based in San Diego, where she advised domestic and international clients on corporate and SEC matters.

Kelly subsequently joined a small boutique law firm in San Diego with a practice in intellectual property law. She covered everything from general corporate counseling to legal advice on offshore transactions.

Kelly has a bachelor's degree in business administration and international relations from California State University, Hayward. She also earned a Bachelor of Laws (LL.B. with honors) from the University of Wales, Swansea, and a Master of Laws (LL.M) from Whittier Law School.

Kelly has successfully founded Bagla Law Firm, APC and loves advising business owners on the Legal Lifecycle of their business.

Kelly and her husband, Brent, live in San Diego with their five dogs.

49407496R00086

Made in the USA
San Bernardino, CA
23 May 2017